Connecting
—————— the ——————
Continents
Heart's Content and the Atlantic Cable

© 2009, Ted Rowe

Newfoundland
Labrador

We gratefully acknowledge the financial support of the Canada Council for the Arts, the Government of Canada through the Book Publishing Industry Development Program (BPIDP), and the Government of Newfoundland and Labrador through the Department of Tourism, Culture and Recreation for our publishing program.

Cover Design by Todd Manning
Layout by Joanne Snook-Hann
Maps and original illustrations by Albert W. Taylor
Cover photo courtesy of Claude Rockwood
Printed on acid-free paper

Published by
CREATIVE PUBLISHERS
an imprint of CREATIVE BOOK PUBLISHING
a Transcontinental Inc. associated company
P.O. Box 8660, Stn. A
St. John's, Newfoundland and Labrador A1B 3T7

Printed in Canada by:
TRANSCONTINENTAL INC.

Rowe, Ted
    Connecting the continents : Heart's Content and the Atlantic cable / Ted Rowe.

ISBN 978-1-897174-42-5

1. Transatlantic cables--History. 2. Telegraph--Newfoundland and Labrador--History. 3. Telegraph stations--Newfoundland and Labrador--Heart's Content--History. 4. Heart's Content (N.L.)--History. I. Title.

TK5611.R69 2009   384.109718   C2009-900593-X

Connecting
—— the ——
Continents
Heart's Content and the Atlantic Cable

Ted Rowe

CREATIVE PUBLISHERS

St. John's, Newfoundland and Labrador
2009

For: Maureen

and

John

Michael

Christopher, Asta &
Rama Alexander

David

Andrew

You are my life.

Table of Contents

Foreword vi

Chapter 1 Frederic Gisborne, Cyrus Field and the Atlantic
           Cable of 1858 2

Chapter 2 Heart's Content 17

Chapter 3 "And there was no more sea" 27

Chapter 4 Communications Outpost 43

Chapter 5 Letters from Sam 55

Chapter 6 Company Town 65

Chapter 7 Higher Standards 75

Chapter 8 Exalted Aspirations 83

Chapter 9 Sport, Art and Hard Living 99

Chapter 10 Hunkering Down 111

Chapter 11 Boom Times 121

Chapter 12 Final Days 131

Postscript 143

Acknowledgements 147

Abbreviations 148

Endnotes 149

Selected Bibliography 157

Foreword

Growing up in Heart's Content in the 1950's, unless your father worked at the cable station you probably never got to see inside the door. I remember going there twice. The first time I was eleven and curious to find out what went on in the old red-brick building off limits to all but a few. I nagged my father until he took me in one Wednesday afternoon when our store was closed for the weekly half-holiday. The men on duty were delighted to welcome visitors and well accustomed to the tour routine. We went into the one-room library, with its polished reading tables and more books stacked in the floor-to-ceiling bookcases than I had ever seen. I saw the billiard room with the heavy old green-baize table and the card room where the men played poker after hours. I was in awe of the array of equipment clicking and humming away in the office, especially when one of the operators had me stand by a machine to see a message welcoming me to the station print out like magic on a ribbon of paper tape. I held on to it as a keepsake for years after.

My second visit was in 1961, on a tour arranged for a group of us in the final year of high school. This time it was more formal, as the staff pointed out how the messages came into the station and passed through the automatic regenerating equipment on their way to New York. We encountered the old-style decorum of the place head-on when we were ushered into the superintendent's office at the end. One of the boys was wearing a cap. "Take your cap off, boy." were his first words. "You don't come into this office with your cap on."

As an example of man's derring-do, perseverance and engineering skill, the completion of the Atlantic cable has few parallels. The events leading up to the cable laying, fraught with challenges and disappointments, is recounted in these pages from a Newfoundland perspective. When the cable came ashore at Heart's Content on July 27, 1866, the relation between the Old and New Worlds changed forever. The news of the day, the price of commodities, government business and private correspondence zipped back and forth beneath the ocean. The endless send-and-receive funnelled through the hands of a select group of telegraphers in a hillside station at Heart's Content, the first of many installed at remote locations as submarine cables circled the globe.

Heart's Content 1940. *Courtesy Crown Lands Photo and Map Library, Province of Newfoundland and Labrador*

Life at the cable station and its impact on an out-of-the-way fishing village is the focus of this book. The cable adventurers who came over from England to operate the station faced hardships of their own, but maintained their lifestyle and culture and developed a society alongside the outport way of life. In the process, they reshaped the educational, religious and social life of the community. They introduced leisure-time activities in music, art, drama and sport. At its peak the station employed over 200 skilled workers in a town of 1,500. For three generations it was a pivotal point in international communications and the focal point of Heart's Content, giving it a flavour and character all its own among the outports of Newfoundland.

Heart's Content today is a quiet place, its population hovering around 400. But go there and you'll find a difference. You'll notice its large, comfortable harbour, more befitting a commercial shipping port than a modest fishing village. You'll see examples of Victorian architecture, rare in rural Newfoundland, and well-to-do housing from the 1920s. The cable station, now an historic site, remains the centrepiece of the town, where thousands of people come each summer to experience a piece of communications history. Here is the story of how it all came about.

A word about the notes, which I have used to document sources, not to supplement the text. Unless you are interested in checking the sources as you read, you can safely ignore the notes without fear of missing anything relevant to the story.

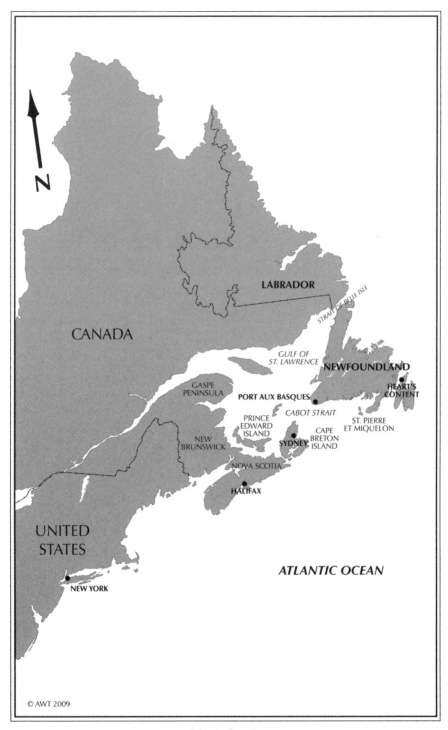

Atlantic Canada

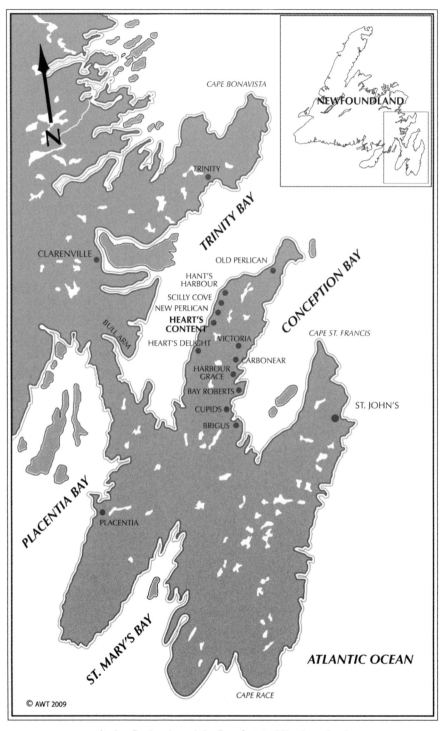

Avalon Peninsula and the East Coast of Newfoundland

Chapter 1

Frederic Gisborne, Cyrus Field and the Atlantic Cable of 1858

The middle of the nineteenth century was an exciting time to be alive. The world was evolving at a rapid clip as Western Europe and North America progressed through the new industrial age. Mechanization was boosting farm production. Manufacturing was replacing manual labour and, in the process, drawing people from the countryside to urban centers. London and New York struggled to keep up with the challenges of a bulging population. The steamship and the steam locomotive rewrote the rules of transportation, moving people from place to place at unprecedented speed, and delivering a wide variety of goods to new consumer markets. Inventions like the kitchen stove, the ice cooler, safety matches, the sewing machine and the gas lamp were within the reach of ordinary people. A series of "World's Fairs," beginning with the London Exhibition of 1851, showcased the strides being made to millions of visitors. For the first time, individuals witnessed significant change within their own lifetimes, change that accelerated as the decades passed. It was an age infatuated with the concept of "progress," glorifying science and industry for the lifestyle enhancements they brought.

The harnessing of electricity brought a new era of communication to this modern world. Optical telegraph systems that signalled by semaphore from hilltop to hilltop gave way to technology unconstrained by physical distance. In 1837 British physicist Charles Wheatstone and medical school dropout William F. Cooke patented an electric telegraph and saw their innovation sweep across Europe. In the United States, artist-turned-inventor Samuel F.B. Morse and Joseph Henry collaborated on a North American version, based on a simple single-key sender. A decade after its introduction in 1844, telegraph lines crisscrossed the eastern United States. Before the next decade was out, they spanned the continent from the Atlantic to the Pacific.

Meanwhile, others were at work on the development of undersea telegraphy. Morse had shown its feasibility as early as 1842, with a submerged cable across New York harbour. Practical application proved tricky, however, because of the little-understood electrical properties of telegraph wire suspended in water, especially over long distances.

Submarine telegraphy showed limited advancement until engineers learned how to compensate for cross induction between the copper wire and the briny sea environment that slowed and garbled the electrical impulses. In England, a company headed by John Brett, a retired antiques dealer, and his brother Jacob, an engineer, installed a 25-mile cable between Dover and Calais, France in 1850. Signalling on the line was erratic and unintelligible. It shut down altogether when a French fisherman snagged the wire, brought it to the surface and cut out a section as a keepsake. Fishermen and cables, it turned out, were destined to have an uneasy coexistence. A hundred years later, cable repairers were busy patching up damage from deep-sea draggers on both sides of the Atlantic. Memento-seeking fishermen aside, the Bretts' first attempt was followed in 1851 by a serviceable cable across the English Channel. Within a few years, England was connected with Ireland and Holland, and undersea cables linked countries in Northern Europe and the Mediterranean.

The looming challenge was to span the North Atlantic. Here the speed of communication was still tied to the speed of transportation, which from London, the centre of world affairs, to New York was about two weeks. A telegraphic connection between the two continents was destined to be a world-altering event. To the Victorian mind it represented the epitome of scientific and engineering accomplishment.

Of course the idea was not lost on visionaries of the day. Samuel Morse, as he was fond of reminding everyone, first raised the prospect of transatlantic communication in 1843. A few years later John and Jacob Brett went so far as to charter a company, a little ahead of their time, for the express purpose of completing a transatlantic cable. In Newfoundland, Bishop John T. Mullock, writing in the *Morning Courier* of St. John's in November 1850, mused, "I hope the day is not too far distant when St. John's will be the first link in the electric chain which will unite the Old World and the New."

It fell to Frederic Newton Gisborne to begin the groundwork for the greatest engineering feat of the century. A dilettante, tinkerer and promoter, Gisborne was born into an upper-class Lancashire family in 1824 (his mother was a descendent of Sir Isaac Newton). He was tutored in mathematics, electricity, botany and civil engineering, and as a young man set out on a world tour that took him to Central and South America and the South Pacific. He and his brother ended up in Quebec in 1845 where they began farming but were soon drawn to the world of telegraphy. Gisborne's early education had prepared him well, and he became part of a company put together to build a line between Quebec and the Maritime provinces. To that end, he traveled to Nova Scotia in the winter of 1848 to seek the backing of the local authorities. His return trek on snowshoes, dragging a loaded toboggan through the rugged mountains of Gaspé, won the admiration of his associates for his courage and extraordinary physical stamina in the wild.

Frederick N. Gisborne (1824-1892). *Courtesy Victoria University Library (Toronto).*

Next year Gisborne moved to Nova Scotia to become superintendent of the colony's telegraph. It was not long before his thoughts turned toward Europe, or at least to Newfoundland. Perhaps influenced by Bishop Mullock's musings, he fixed on the idea of a telegraph connecting St. John's, the closest seaport to Europe, to eastern North America. Establishing St. John's as the first port of call for ships crossing the Atlantic would cut the communication time between London and New York by two days, a significant improvement in a world now hungry for up-to-the-minute information. Gisborne proposed to build a telegraph line from St. John's across the south coast of Newfoundland to Cape Ray on the southwest tip. His plan then was to ferry messages to Cape Breton by boat or carrier pigeon. With news of the Bretts' English Channel cable, however, a submarine cable across the Cabot Strait became a workable alternative.

Gisborne came to St. John's in late 1850 and generated considerable interest in his scheme to make the colony the point of connection for transatlantic communication. He in turn found himself captivated by the island and puzzled by the prevailing opinion on the mainland depicting it as a desolate, backward place good only for codfish. Gisborne saw a land of vast natural resources whose inhospitable shores shielded behind them "as warm-hearted and intelligent a population as ever breathed."[1] He resigned his position with the Nova Scotia government and, with a new 15-year-old wife in tow, took up residence in St. John's in the summer of 1851.

He chartered the Newfoundland Electric Telegraph Company and started work on a telegraph line from St. John's to Carbonear. With that project in hand, he left in the fall to survey the 350-mile route to

Cape Ray. It was a gruelling two-month journey that took him across some of the most challenging terrain in North America, detouring around long, steep-sided inlets, hampered by inaccurate charts and cold wet weather, and living for days on a subsistence diet of bread and tea. The expedition tested even Gisborne's prowess in the wild. His party of six quickly lost heart but Gisborne was not about to quit. Stopping for supplies at the Mi'kmaq settlement of Conne River, Gisborne partied with the natives, giving them great amusement at the sight of the bald, bearded Englishman demonstrating gymnastic exercises and New Zealand and Tahitian war dances. His men eventually deserted him, to be replaced by four Mi'kmaq better suited to the rigours of the outdoors. Slogging 10-12 miles a day when the weather allowed, the Indians were awestruck at Gisborne's endurance. Before long two of them turned back. One of the two who completed the trek to Cape Ray died within a few days, and the other never fully recovered from the experience.

The survey complete, Gisborne took but a short pause in St. John's before heading to New York to arrange financial backing for the telegraph line. Then it was off to England to consult with John Brett on the submarine connection between Newfoundland and Cape Breton. Brett also offered financial support and was eager to talk about a partnership for a transatlantic cable. Gisborne, however, wanted to complete the Newfoundland line before tackling the Atlantic. Returning to St. John's, he chartered the Newfoundland Electric Telegraph Company with exclusive rights to build and operate a trans-island telegraph. The Nova Scotia government put an exorbitant price on landing rights for a cable from Newfoundland, so he decided to bypass them with a route to New Brunswick via Prince Edward Island. He completed the 10-mile section from P.E.I. to New Brunswick toward the end of 1852, the first working submarine cable in North America.

Back in Newfoundland the following year, he began work on the line across the island. Unfortunately Gisborne, while sharp on telegraphy and a superb outdoorsman, was naïve and none too practical when it came to matters of business. In August the project came to an abrupt halt when his New York backers refused to honour his payment requests. Only 40 miles of line had been completed, the workers were clamouring for their wages and suppliers were demanding to be paid. His funds exhausted, Gisborne suffered the humiliation of having his personal property seized. He was placed under arrest, and it was only the intervention of two acquaintances from P.E.I. in arranging bail

Cyrus W. Field (1819-1892).
From McDonald (1937).

that spared him a prison term. In the midst of the chaos, he suffered the sudden death of his young wife, leaving two small children in his care. Despite the setbacks, in January 1854 he left again for New York in search of new financing.[2] He was convinced he had a viable project, and John Brett was still holding out the promise of a partnership in an Atlantic cable. All Gisborne needed was someone to help him pull it off. That someone was Cyrus Field.

Bright, ambitious, and possessed of a restless energy, Cyrus West Field grew up in Stockbridge, Massachusetts, the son of David Dudley Field, a well-known and highly regarded Congregational minister. By any measure, his was an extraordinary family, with five sons going on to achieve distinction in law, politics, engineering and the ministry. Cyrus, born in 1819, shunned the halls of higher learning for a career in business, making his way at the age of 16 to the financial and business capital of America, New York City. He moved up the business ladder, eventually taking control of a wholesale paper firm and building it into one of the most successful paper and printing supply wholesalers in the country. Within a decade he counted himself among the wealthiest men in New York.

In 1853, still only 33 years old but with the pressures of business taking their toll, Field prepared for a life of semi-retirement. That all changed, however, when he met Frederic Gisborne. A chance encounter with Matthew Field, the engineer of the family, in February 1854 brought Gisborne to Cyrus Field's swank East Side townhouse at Gramercy Park. Hearing what Gisborne had to say, Field was not particularly enthusiastic about investing in a telegraph link between St. John's and the rest of North America. Cyrus Field's brother Henry, author of an early account of the transatlantic cable, related that after Gisborne left, Field looked up Newfoundland's position on the globe, saw how close it was to Britain and was struck with the notion of a cable extending across the Atlantic. The anecdote is part of cable history, crediting Field with the initial idea as well as its execution. Gisborne had a different version of the meeting. According to him, the two openly discussed a transatlantic cable.[3] D.J. Henderson of St. John's, also present at the meeting, later recalled that Gisborne, in pitching his case, produced a map tracing a proposed cable route between Newfoundland and Ireland. "Ah," said Field, "that puts a different complexion on the whole thing."[4]

Indeed it did, and Field moved quickly to put the idea into action. He assembled a group of New York investors, all men of wealth and influence, and in March 1854 formed the New York, Newfoundland and London Telegraph Company, with Gisborne as Chief Engineer. The dream of a working cable across the Atlantic became Cyrus Field's consuming passion for the next 12 years.

Field and Gisborne set out for St. John's, accompanied by brother David Dudley Field, the company's legal advisor, and one of the investors, Chandler White. They arrived on March 22 after a storm-tossed, stomach-churning passage from Halifax. Cyrus Field, prone to seasickness, was more than a little the worse for wear. Fortunately for him, the Legislative Assembly of Newfoundland, about to introduce responsible government to the colony, was quick to respond to interest from outside promoters. In a matter of days they agreed to the company's terms: guaranteed interest on a £250,000 bond for 20 years, no duty on the import of wires and cables, £5,000 for road construction, a grant of 50 square miles of land upon completion of the telegraph to the mainland, a further 50 square miles upon completion of the Atlantic telegraph, and, most critically, a 50-year monopoly on telegraphic communication in the colony.

The Americans paid Gisborne $40,000 for the assets of the his bankrupt company, assumed its $50,000 debt and took charge. They settled the wages of the workers from the year before, and that summer geared up again with a crew of 600. Chandler White moved to St. John's as the company's managing director. Gisborne was shunted aside. He did not get along with White, who ignored his advice as Chief Engineer, and he resigned. Matthew Field took over construction of the telegraph line. It was hard going, even for an experienced engineer, and the costs escalated wildly. The following spring, Cyrus Field, with his characteristic impatience, wanted to know how many more months it would take to finish the line. "How many months?" replied Matthew. "Let's say how many years!"[5]

The company pushed ahead, meantime, with the undersea cable to the mainland. By now the Nova Scotia government had come to terms on a landing site in Cape Breton. With cable-laying technology still in its infancy, this phase of the project started out badly. Cyrus Field was in a hurry to get started but knew next to nothing about how to proceed. Early in 1855, with an introduction from Gisborne, he enlisted the help of John Brett in arranging for the manufacture of the cable in England and engaged the 500-ton brig *Sarah L. Bryant* to bring it to Newfoundland the following summer. He also hired Samuel Canning, a bright young engineer associated with Brett, to head up the project. Laying the cable could not be accomplished under sail power, so Field chartered the steamer *James Adger* in New York to tow the *Sarah L. Bryant* across the 55 miles of the Cabot Strait as she put the cable down.

By August 1855 all was ready, and the *James Adger* left New York with Cyrus Field and other principals of the New York, Newfoundland and London Telegraph Company on board. Many of them brought their families along. To promote the event, Field also invited an assortment of friends, luminaries and newspaper reporters, giving the expedition the atmosphere of a grand sea cruise. Coming into Port aux Basques, the troupe found that the *Sarah L. Bryant* was yet to arrive from England. Off they went on a side trip to St. John's, where the Americans were quite taken by the hospitality of the Newfoundlanders, and no less so by the number of Newfoundland dogs they saw roaming the streets. They left with 20 of them on board, on their way to new homes in the United States. The dogs came in handy back at Cape Ray where Samuel Canning, the engineer in charge, was making preparations to secure the Newfoundland end of the cable. In trying to land a supply of lumber to build a telegraph shack, much of it broke free in the crashing surf. Over the side went the large, web-footed Newfoundland retrievers. Working individually and in pairs, the dogs delighted their new owners as they brought ashore each and every board.

The cable-laying operation was a disaster. The *Sarah L. Bryant* had no sooner started paying out the cable than she was struck broadside by the *James Adger*, whose captain, a disagreeable man named Turner, had been slighted by Cyrus Field at the dinner table. When the towing resumed, Turner steadfastly refused to take direction from Field or anyone else. He took the steamer far off course, then overcorrected, and failed to adjust his speed to the brig. As a result, the excess weight of the cable dragged the *Sarah L. Bryant* down in the stern. When the weather turned foul, with gale force winds and a rising sea, there was no choice but to cut the cable and abandon the project. It was a humiliation for Field and his partners, but their spirits were not completely dashed. As the *James Adger* steamed towards home,

Newfoundland dogs and all, they hosted a final costume ball for their guests the night before docking in New York.

Next summer there was no partying. The steamer *Propontis* laid the Cabot Strait cable without incident under the eye of Samuel Canning. Meanwhile, construction of the trans-island line was lagging badly. Matthew Field had been replaced as engineer in charge, but almost two-thirds of the line was yet to be completed. There was one man who could finish the job and that was Frederic Gisborne. On Cyrus Field's offer to involve him in promoting the transatlantic cable in England, Gisborne accepted a reappointment as Chief Engineer in early 1856. By October the line was finished.

The New York, Newfoundland and London Telegraph Company now had a telegraph link from St. John's to New York. They had also spent a lot of money. In fact, their original capital of $1.5 million was almost exhausted, and they had yet to face the real challenge of spanning the Atlantic. Cyrus Field again snubbed Gisborne, starting for England without him. John Brett opened doors for him, and along with engineer Charles T. Bright, and a former surgeon and self-made electrician named Edward Wildman Whitehouse, they set up the Atlantic Telegraph Company to raise the necessary capital. For their board of directors they recruited some of the most illustrious businessmen in Britain, along with William Thomson, a quiet but brilliant Glasgow physicist and mathematician and leading authority on electrical theory. Their initial share issue raised £350,000, the equivalent of US $1,750,000.[6]

The British government came on board, offering naval assistance in laying the cable. Just as important, they committed funds for priority use of the cable once it became operational. A weary Cyrus Field returned to New York to spend Christmas with his family, but at the last minute it dawned on him that Atlantic Telegraph had not secured cable-landing rights in Newfoundland. He made a quick dash to St. John's where the whirlwind schedule caught up with him and he dropped from exhaustion. Ordered to bed by his doctor, he instead caught the next steamer back to New York. A winter of intense lobbying lay ahead to win the support of the US Congress for what was now essentially a British project. The politics were touch and go, but legislation creating a 25-year subsidy for the cable service squeaked through the Senate with a one-vote majority.

Meanwhile, disgusted with his treatment by Field, Frederic Gisborne turned his back on telegraphy, later writing "under the guise of friendship and esteem [Field] has been my worst enemy."[7]   The two finally parted ways. Gisborne stayed in England, returning to Newfoundland in the spring of 1857 to take up mineral exploration. His contribution to telegraphy, however, was not lost on the Newfoundlanders, who within weeks of his arrival in St. John's organized a public dinner in his honour. "To his fertile mind, physical activity, indomitable perseverance, we owe the agency of electricity in our internal as well as foreign associations," wrote *The Public Ledger*.[8]

Back in England the machinery was humming, turning out the 2,500 miles of cable needed for the summer expedition. It was designed with a strand of seven fine copper wires at its core, surrounded by three layers of gutta-percha, the new wonder material pliable under normal temperatures but forming a hard, efficient insulator in cold water. The outside was wrapped with treated hemp and wound with an armour of iron wires, each of seven strands, the whole thing coated with a layer of tar producing a cable just over half an inch in diameter.

There was no ship large enough to carry its entire length, so when the time came it was loaded in two sections on the 5,200-ton USS *Niagara* and the 3,500-ton HMS *Agamemnon*. On August 6, 1857, the specially prepared shore section of the cable, heavily armoured for extra protection against the rocky bottom, was brought ashore from the *Niagara* at Valentia Island in County Kerry, Ireland. The two ships, with an accompanying squadron, departed for Newfoundland. Samuel Canning had selected Bull Arm at the bottom of Trinity Bay as the landing site, where a new telegraph house awaited their arrival. Alexander M. Mackay, a Nova Scotian hired by Cyrus Field as Newfoundland superintendent of the New York, Newfoundland and London Telegraph Company, insured that the trans-island line was in top shape. In St. John's, a special committee laid plans for a public celebration on the arrival of the telegraph fleet.

All through August they waited, not knowing that the expedition had gone awry. On August 11, with 380 miles of cable on the ocean floor behind the *Niagara*, the mechanic tending the paying-out equipment applied the brakes in error and the cable snapped. With no means of retrieving it from a depth of 12,000 feet, the voyage ended and the fleet returned to Britain. News of the expedition's collapse reached St. John's on August 27. Frederic Gisborne, now in the position of Colonial Telegraph Engineer in Newfoundland, had predicted the failure. He contacted Atlantic Telegraph to offer his services, proposing that if appointed Chief Engineer with full powers he would

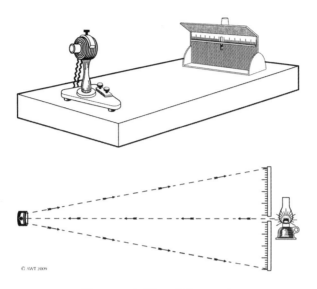

Thompson's Mirror Galvanometer.
Light from the lamp reflects back from the mirror inside the coil
to appear as a spot of light on the graduated scale.

submit a plan for laying the cable and be prepared to forfeit £1,000 if it failed.[9] He was ignored.

Two more attempts in 1858, where the ships were pounded by fierce mid-Atlantic storms, both ended with fatal breaks in the cable. Finally, in July, the *Agamemnon* and the *Niagara* set out again, this time splicing the cable at mid-Atlantic.   The *Agamemnon*, carrying Charles Bright, William Thomson and Samuel Canning, headed back to Ireland, and the *Niagara*, with Field and electrician Charles de Sauty on board, set course for Newfoundland. On this voyage cable communication from ship to shore was much improved by new equipment provided by William Thomson. A troublesome problem with submarine telegraphy was the progressive weakening of the signal as the length of the cable increased. Thomson came up with a solution one day as he sat idly twirling his monocle, watching the refracted beam of sunlight dance around the room. The thought struck him that a light source might be adapted to amplify the faint cable signals. He proceeded to fashion a device with a small mirror suspended inside an electrical coil. A tiny magnet fixed to the back of the mirror caused it to rotate to the left or right in response to a positive or negative electrical signal. Directing a beam of light at the mirror from an oil lamp reflected a spot of light onto a graduated scale that in turn moved left or right in response to the signals. The mirror galvanometer became the standard instrument for reading code on ocean cables until the siphon galvanometer, another Thomson invention that produced a written record on a moving paper tape, came along in the 1870s.

The latest cable expedition produced some hair-raising moments of lost signals, damaged cable, false compass readings, and fuel shortages, but no breaks in the line. Both ships approached their destinations within hours of each other on Wednesday, August 4th – the *Agamemnon* at Valentia and the *Niagara* at Trinity Bay. As the *Niagara* cruised slowly toward Bull Arm accompanied by HMS *Gorgon* and HMS *Porcupine*, Cyrus Field's impatience got the better of him and he transferred to the *Gorgon* to go on ahead. He landed at 2 a.m. and struck out for the telegraph house a half-mile from the shore. There he roused the men from their sleep with word that the cable was laid but there was no operator among them to send out the news. Field cooled his heels while two of the workers hurried off to the nearest station 15 miles away at Black River (near present-day Swift Current) with a dispatch to the Associated Press in New York.

Meanwhile, the crew of the *Niagara* was busy coiling the last length of cable, some one-and-a-half miles long, into a landing boat. By early dawn they were on the beach and men from the *Gorgon* and *Porcupine* converged on the site. Sailors and officers alike pitched in to form a procession along the tar-covered cable, grasping it in their bare hands and dragging it inland over the rough bridle path to the telegraph house. Once there, the end hooked up to the receiving instrument, clear signals from Valentia were confirmed. Outside, the men stood around as Captain W. Hudson of the *Niagara* marked the occasion with a brief address and a prayer of thanks. Back at the beach they could contain themselves no longer, and in the words of John Mullaly, the self-styled historian of the expedition, raised their cheers as "one wild prolonged shout of delirious joy."[10]

The whole of America celebrated the news of the cable landing. All over, jubilation was the order of the day. "…we cannot but admit the achievement as a testimonial of the remarkable eminence to which science has attained, eclipsing everything of which the skill and ingenuity of the past can boast" applauded *The Public Ledger* on August 6. Arriving at St. John's on Monday evening en route to New York, the *Niagara* and *Gorgon* were greeted by the firing of guns, ringing of church bells and a display of fireworks. Public buildings, banks and numerous private residences were brightly lit, and people thronged the streets as a surge of excitement ran through the city. The following evening Cyrus Field and the ships' officers were entertained by the governor at dinner and feted at a ball at the Colonial Building. Captain Hudson of the *Niagara* commented, "Newfoundland took the first part in it, and Great Britain and America joined her, and now she is the very heart and focus through which their current of union runs – truly a proud position..."[11]

Cyrus Field arrived in New York to a hero's welcome. Two days of celebration included a parade up Broadway with Field beaming and bowing from the mayor's carriage. The whole city partied and couples danced to the latest popular tune, "The Atlantic Telegraph Polka."

As far as the Newfoundlanders were concerned, there was something missing in all the hoopla, and that was the recognition of Frederic Gisborne's contribution. The St. John's press took up his cause, publishing correspondence between him and John Brett that clearly anticipated an ocean telegraph long before Field's involvement. While acknowledging that "it would be unjust and ungenerous to detract one iota" from the honour belonging to Cyrus Field, *The Public Ledger* posed the question:

> ...who *was* the projector of this great plan of uniting the nations of the earth? Most assuredly it was not the man who accomplished it. It is to be regretted that the pioneer in this adventure has been completely set aside, and no notice whatever taken of his extraordinary exertions in its inception, except in an equivocal manner. The paternity of this great work belongs to FREDERICK N. GISBORNE, Esq., whose claims in this respect have been so fully borne out long since that a repetition now is needless...it will be admitted by the whole community that to his first ideas and perseverance under many difficulties are we now indebted for the completion of the connection of both worlds.[12]

Controversy over Gisborne's role reached the New York papers, where there was no inclination to assign any credit but to one of their own. The principals of the New York, Newfoundland and London Telegraph Company, in a statement defending their claim to the project, argued rather lamely that the charter of Gisborne's original Newfoundland Electric Telegraph Company made no reference to an Atlantic cable.[13] St. John's continued to champion Gisborne, condemning the "manifest untruth" foisted upon the world by "the Yankee Cyrus" to further his own ends.[14]

In the meantime, after some initial testing and instrument adjustments, the cable was ready to accept business on August 16. Wildman Whitehouse supervised the operation at Valentia, and Charles de Sauty oversaw the lonely outpost in Bull Arm. Official messages were exchanged between Queen Victoria and US President James Buchanan, followed by several hundred dispatches over the next two weeks, but the service was not working well. At both ends, transmission was slow and the incoming signals weak and hard to interpret. The company dispatched a second electrician, Charles W. Lundy, to Newfoundland but there was little he could do. On September 2, less than a month after the cable landed, and the very day that Field was honoured at a grand banquet in New York, Bull Arm received its last legible message. Another six weeks of static and the line went dead.

Cyrus Field shouldered the blame. Accusations flew that the whole cable project was a fraud, that Field had faked the messages just to profit from the sale of his shares. The fact that he had sold just one share in the company - and that at a loss - made no difference. Opinion went against him; friends and business associates who had made him the man of the hour only a month before turned their backs. It would take him years to restore public confidence in himself and the idea of a transatlantic cable.

What caused the cable to fail? Field's impatience to get the project underway led to some hasty preparations, and there were inherent defects in the cable stemming from shoddy manufacturing and storage. However, a public inquiry focussed on Atlantic's chief electrician, Wildman Whitehouse, whose renegade actions in this instance lent credence to his name. Even though William Thomson had demonstrated that signals could be driven through the length of the cable by applying only a small amount of voltage, Whitehouse, with a lesser grasp of electrical principles and a blustery, pig-headed disposition, insisted that stronger signals required more juice. He had a series of huge induction coils set up at Valentia capable of generating as much as 2,000 volts, and as the signals weakened applied more and more power. The inquiry concluded that his transmissions were strong enough to burn through the gutta-percha insulation and short out the cable.

Despite the personal attacks and a reversal of fortune in his own business, Cyrus Field continued to tout the cable project. With civil war raging in the United States, investor support for a new attempt at cable laying was meagre. In the meantime, the Associated Press news service intercepted transatlantic news in Newfoundland, not at St. John's as Field had planned, but with a small boat bobbing around in the waters off Cape Race. Ocean steamers bound for America threw the news over the side in watertight containers, to be ferried in to the telegraph station and sent on to New York.

Cyrus Field again took his fundraising efforts to England, and again it paid off. By early 1864, he had new investors breathing life into the project. Industrialist Daniel Gooch was among them. He brought not only money and business expertise, but also a means of getting a new cable across the Atlantic. Gooch headed a consortium that owned the steamship *Great Eastern*. Launched in 1858, at a length of 693 feet with 22,500 tons displacement, the *Great Eastern* was a marvel of her time. Next to the *Titanic* at 46,000 tons or today's giant cruise ships that regularly exceed 100,000 tons she would not be impressive, but she dwarfed all other ships of her day. Fitted with six masts carrying well over an acre of canvas, two side paddles and a single screw, the *Great Eastern* was, in fact, so large as to be commercially useless and she bankrupted a succession of owners. But she was the only ship afloat that could transport the entire length of newly designed cable weighing over 4,600 tons. Gooch made her available free of charge to Atlantic Telegraph in exchange for £50,000 in stock once the project succeeded. Field lost no time in inking a deal to put her into service.

By the summer of 1864 planning for the new expedition was well advanced and Field hurried back to Newfoundland. The waters of Bull Arm could not accommodate the *Great Eastern*, and the Royal Navy offered him the survey ship *Margaretta Stevenson*, under Captain John Orlebar of Charlottetown, to find a new landing site. Field and Orlebar met up in St. John's, dined with the Governor, and set out for Trinity Bay. Field found some time to collect biological specimens for his friend Louis Agassiz of the Harvard Museum of Comparative Zoology. Orlebar, meanwhile, turned to the survey work. He had earlier favoured New Perlican, but with the *Great Eastern* commissioned to lay the cable the deep, spacious harbour at Heart's Content proved much more attractive:

> ...in view of the *Great Eastern* being employed to lay the cable, I have now surveyed [Heart's Content], and find it very superior to New Perlican. Heart's Content contains a population of 654 persons, principally

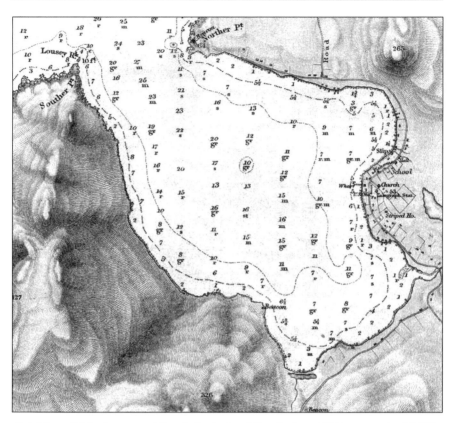

Detail from Orlebar's survey of Heart's Content and New Perlican (1864, map revised 1873). Published at the Admiralty March 1, 1865. *Courtesy National Archive, London.*

engaged in the fisheries, and nearly all belonging to the Church of England. The Church and Village stand on the East side of the Harbour, with a Parsonage and large Schoolhouse near. There is a resident Clergyman who is supported entirely by the people, and a School Master, partly paid by the Colonial and Continental Church Society and partly by the Newfoundland Board of Education. A well-travelled and tolerable carriage road connects Heart's Content with Harbour Grace, 15 miles distant, and St. John's, 81 miles distant.[15]

There was no argument from Cyrus Field. The name alone foretold success. Heart's Content was where the cable would come ashore.

Chapter 2

Heart's Content

There they have been living, generation after generation, in this obscure and bleak region, hidden behind
their fogs and rocky barriers from the rude gaze of the
great world beyond, doing and thinking and believing,
as their fathers and excellent old grannies had done
and believed from time out of mind before them,
knowing little and caring less for the wonders of modern thought and miracles of modern achievement,
when, suddenly, one fine morning, the [*Great Eastern*]
dropped into their harbour with the Nineteenth
Century in its hold done up in a hempen rope.[1]

To the people of Heart's Content, steeped in the tradition of the
fishery, the prospect of becoming the North American portal for
transatlantic communication must have come as a sobering thought.
The contrast with their existing way of life could hardly have been
more pronounced. The cable represented the high technology of its
day, requiring skilled operators trained on specialized equipment
working around the clock to relay information from one side of the
ocean to the other. The whole notion was foreign to Heart's Content,
which as far as communication was concerned had not even so much
as a post office.

Consider as well that in the 1860s the Newfoundland fishery was at
a low ebb. Throughout the colony an unnatural change in the ocean
waters was proving disastrous for the cod. Years later older fishermen
recalled the unusual conditions. For some reason the water was
strangely clear, where they could see bottom in 20 fathoms, but their
nets were coated with a filthy slime. It was an environment that the
cod could not live in, and they all but disappeared from inshore
waters.[2] The spring seal fishery, which offered a little income to fishing families after the long winter, was also in a slump, yielding half the
number of seals as the previous decade. The situation was so desperate that one-quarter of government spending was going toward poor
relief to supply rations of corn meal and molasses to the destitute.
Heart's Content had some reprieve from a small shipbuilding indus-

try where men turned out wooden brigs and schooners for the fishery and merchant trading, but in the main the people depended on the cod, and the cod were staying away.

It wasn't always so. Like other settlements along the east coast of the island, the community had its beginnings as a seasonal fishing station for seamen from the West Country of England, sailing from Devon, Dorset and Somerset to work the cod-rich waters of Newfoundland. By the early 1600s they were coming by the thousands, arriving in the spring and staying until the late August sunsets flared the sky and the nights began to cool. Every day they fished with baited hooks from open boats, cleaning, splitting, salting and drying their catch on shore. Like the men, the accommodations were rough and ready. Wharves and sheds (stages) were thrown together from rough-hewn local timber, as were the large rickety platforms for drying the fish (flakes), and the sleeping huts (tilts) for the men and boys. When the fishermen left, the ship loaded down with salt cod and casks of cod liver oil, the makeshift station faced the storms of winter and foraging from the native Beothuk. Likely as not, whoever came next year would have to start all over again.

One of the early fishing captains to sail into the large sheltered harbour destined to receive the Atlantic cable saw two coves broadening out from its entrance like the two halves of a heart. From this, tradition has it, came the name Heart's Content. By 1612 it was known to John Guy, founder of Newfoundland's first colony at Cupids. On an exploration voyage of Trinity Bay, Guy's party put into Heart's Content and reported "an excellent good place for fishing for some 8 ships."[3]

A good place for fishing perhaps, but settlement was slow to take hold. It is not until 1679 that we find mention of a fisherman staying through the winter. John Bennet stayed only a year or two at that. So did several others who came the following year. Like most of the early settlers (or planters as they were called) they tended to move around in search of richer fishing grounds, and in the closing decades of the 1600s a number of them drifted in and out of Heart's Content. Some put up makeshift premises in the style of the ship fishermen (a fishing room) or took over their abandoned buildings, living in simple little one-room tilts of upright sticks chinked with moss. The accommodations offered little comfort. With tiny unglazed windows and only a hole for a chimney, tilts were inclined to fill with smoke from the fire on the open stone hearth. In Newfoundland today, a heavy smoker is still said to "smoke like a tilt." Other planters built more permanent quarters, modeled after the peasant cottages of the West Country. They brought in hired hands (servants) from the poor villages of England and Ireland, to help with the fishing. Their plantation (far too grand a word perhaps, not meant to conjure up images of colonial Virginia) was a strip of beachfront property with a stage, a few store-rooms and flakes, a small garden set with turnip and cabbage (pota-toes were not introduced until the middle of the next century), and perhaps space for a few animals.

The eighteenth century brought the nucleus of a permanent popu-lation. By 1753 the community was home to 11 families, three single planters, 57 servants and a population of 91.[4] The ship fishery was waning and the Heart's Content planters traded fish for supplies with British merchant firms represented in Trinity, a bustling commercial center and headquarters for the fishery on the Northeast coast of Newfoundland. They conducted business on credit, through the sys-tem of "truck," or commodity exchange that had grown up in Newfoundland. In the spring the merchant advanced fishing gear, food, clothing and other provisions to the planters, who made pay-ment in the fall in fish and other commodities such as oil, sealskins, furs or lumber. If payment fell short of the value of the goods advanced, the merchant carried over the difference to the next sea-son. It was a business arrangement that more resembled a master-ser-vant relationship, with the Newfoundlanders held in the tight grip of their British overseers.

Into this scantly educated, merchant-dominated backwoods came the clergy, sponsored by the Society for the Propagation of the Gospel, the missionary arm of the Church of England. They were not always well received, especially by the merchants, for whom the prospect of consciousness raising and increased literacy presented a threat to the truck system. Heart's Content saw its first missionary in the 1760s, when Reverend James Balfour, an amiable ex-Presbyterian stationed at Trinity, began coming around in the early fall, as the fishing was wind-ing down, to preach, baptize and marry. He was appalled at the state of ignorance in the outharbours of Trinity Bay. At Heart's Content a woman presented herself to be baptized, he reported in dismay, with no knowledge of "who made this world or redeemed mankind."[5] In a few years, however, Balfour saw some results for his efforts in that one man who could read a little began holding church services. Methodism was also spreading through the outports from a charismatic ministry founded in Harbour Grace by Irishman Laurence Coughlan, a disciple of John Wesley, but the movement garnered little support in Heart's Content.

As the nineteenth century dawned, a soaring demand for salt cod on the international market provided an economic boom in Newfoundland. At the same time, a market developed for Newfoundland seal oil to light the lamps of Europe. Heart's Content advanced with the prosperous times. Mainstay families like Langer, Piercey, Sinyard, Sooley, Rockwood, Rowe, Moore, Hopkins, Legge, Cumby and George occupied fishing rooms around the harbour. Joseph Burrage, a sea captain and merchant from Trinity, opened a general provisions store. A shipyard operated by the Rowes turned into a busy little enterprise building brigs for the new Newfoundland merchant class, along with fishing schooners for sealing and a growing summer fishery on the coast of Labrador. The Hopkins family began a lucrative trade in the cod fishery, sealing and shipbuilding. Commerce received an added boost with the arrival of two enterprising men from St. John's, Richard Underhay and British-born Robert Ollerhead, who established plantations next door to each other on the point in the centre of the harbour.

Underhay, a devout Church of England man, had the first church built around 1820, on the hill behind his plantation. He conducted church services between visits of the missionary from Trinity and also started a Sunday school where children could learn the rudiments of reading and writing, catechism and Bible text. In 1828 the first day-school opened using the church as a schoolroom, and accommodating up to 50 children under schoolmaster James Moore, one of the few qualified men around, having clerked in Joseph Burrage's store. The day-school was supported by the Society for the Propagation of the Gospel and, like the Sunday school, had a simple program of instruction heavily weighted toward church teaching. The church itself, now consecrated as St. Mary's, welcomed Deacon Otto Weeks from Nova Scotia as its first clergyman in 1827.

After the early century boom, the 1830s brought a time of hardship and decline. The market for codfish fell drastically and there were widespread failures in the potato crop. Newfoundland's first legislature, opened in 1833, met a flood of petitions for famine relief from all around the coast. On a bare-bones budget, the government dealt with the poor as best they could, while providing funding for health, road building, and policing of outports. Robert Ollerhead became

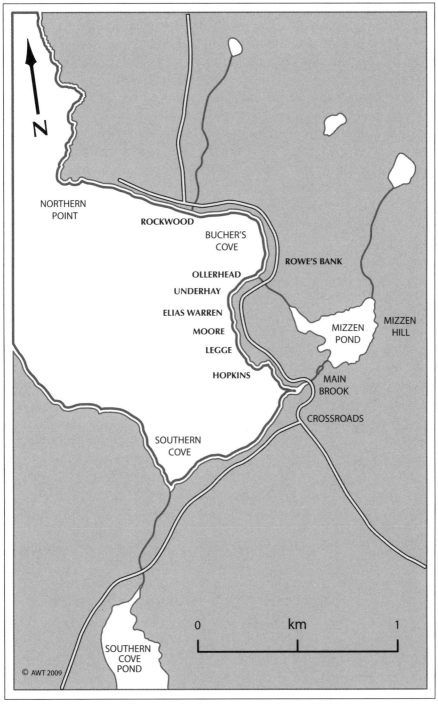

Heart's Content, showing major plantations, c. 1850.

Justice of the Peace for Heart's Content, with blacksmith Charles Rendell as his constable. The community also benefited from government spending on road construction. The ancient footpath across Heart's Content Barrens, the windswept height of land between Heart's Content and Carbonear, was a well-traveled route and one of the first earmarked for improvement. A new road went through in the late 1830s, opening up commerce with Conception Bay.

As the population increased, they outgrew Underhay's church, which was replaced in 1846 during the time of Reverend Henry Lind. Appointed chair of the district Board of Education, Lind also saw to the upgrading of their primitive, little sod-roofed schoolhouse. Around 1860 the church was enlarged to accommodate 587 Church of England parishioners. At the time, the Roman Catholic population numbered 67. No one yet professed to being a Methodist.[6]

By 1858, the old schoolhouse, crammed with 70 children under schoolmaster William Thompson, had also outlived its days. Schooling was now funded by the Colonial and Continental Church Society (CCCS), also affiliated with the Church of England, and it refused to renew its grant to Heart's Content until the people did something about the condition of the school. Thomas Higgins, a Society supporter from Harbour Grace, stepped forward to build a new one. Higgins' charity outshone his construction skills, however, for within a year the building blew down and was nothing but a pile of rubble. The Board of Education replaced it with another, which stayed put.

In 1861, the Mission of Heart's Content, encompassing the settlements of Heart's Delight, New Perlican and Scilly Cove, came under the charge of Rev. George Gardner, a 23-year-old graduate of Queen's Theological College in St. John's. Ten years in Newfoundland, Gardner had come from England with his missionary parents, both teachers with the CCCS. A thoughtful, caring man, always seen in a swallowtail coat and white gloves, he took the chance of a posting at Heart's Content with no guarantee of a stipend from the Society for the Propagation of the Gospel. Given the impoverished state of the fishery, it was a challenge all round: "...this Mission... is one of the two which have voluntarily engaged to wholly support their Clergymen. It is much to be regretted, for his sake and theirs, that at present, in this Mission, they have great difficulty in fulfilling their engagement," noted the *Harbour Grace Standard*.[7]

In his quiet way, however, Gardner was able to marshal the people to build new churches at Heart's Delight and Scilly Cove. At Heart's

Content, he was stirred to action by the plight of the poor fishing families, especially those left destitute by the sickness or death of the father. People were helping each other out as best they could, but Gardner saw the need for a more formal support system. In the villages of England, men had learned to deal with such adversity by organizing themselves into "friendly societies," paying into a pool that provided unemployment, sickness and death benefits for the members. Gardner was not long promoting the idea in Heart's Content.

George Gardner (1838-?).

On a Friday night in February, 1862, about 30 men turned out to a public meeting in the schoolhouse to hear Gardner outline his plan for a benefit club where the members could sustain each other in times of financial need. Outport men needed little persuasion to adopt such a scheme, and before the night was over, they founded the Heart's Content Fishermen's Society with Gardner as President. Membership was open to any man who wanted to join, and in a very short time members flocked in from other communities up and down the shore.

Under Gardner's guidance, the Society swelled to 250 strong, outgrowing the schoolhouse as a meeting place, and in 1869 they built their own hall. Through his gentle guidance, Gardner endeared himself to the membership and the community. However, he was lax in financial matters, and the rapid growth of the Society produced the same problems faced by friendly societies in England - demands for sickness and death benefits that far outstripped revenue from membership dues. Within a few years the Society found itself facing insolvency. Eventually its executive came up with a restructuring scheme, similar to the path followed by the English societies in affiliating with each other to spread the financial risk. In 1873, the Heart's Content Fishermen's Society became the Society of United Fishermen, with a broader membership base and the administrative capacity to deal with expansion demands. Re-energized, the Society expanded rapidly throughout the island and briefly into Nova Scotia. Although its function as a benefit society is long past, it still functions as the only homegrown fraternal organization in Newfoundland.

So we return to 1864, to a settlement struggling to make its way through another downturn in the fishery. Heart's Content now had 120 houses sprinkled around the harbour, with two-storey saltboxes, the latest style of housing, beginning to make an appearance among the older cottages, tilts and plantation homes. The community had also evolved into distinct neighbourhoods. Northern Point (the Point) ended at the Rockwood plantation. Rowe's Bank ran between Butcher's Cove and the Rowe dockyard. The Centre of the Harbour (referred to as "up the harbour" by those who lived to the north and "down the harbour" or "over the harbour" by those to the south) had the largest cluster of homes. A few families lived near the Main Brook (the Brook) and others around the Crossroads, where the road to Carbonear began. At the far end of the harbour, Southern Cove was home to several more.

As the central community on the south side of Trinity Bay, Heart's Content boasted three general dealers.[8] Ridley & Company, prominent merchants of Harbour Grace, operated a branch store. Adjoining the Underhay estate was a plantation owned by Elias Warren, an ambitious Heart's Content-born fisherman and sea captain who had worked his way up to one of the business successes of the community. When the Slade family, successors in business to Joseph Burrage, went insolvent in 1861, he took over their premises in Butcher's Cove. Next door was a business operated by Richard Penney, recently arrived from Carbonear.

Apart from the merchants, George Gardner the revered clergyman, William Thompson the schoolmaster, and magistrate Robert Ollerhead, who died in 1864 at the age of 75, the great bulk of the people were planters or fishermen, catching and curing the cod the same way their predecessors had centuries before. The level of literacy was modest, especially among the older people who could still remember a time when there was no church or school. The planters owned the more substantial fishing premises, working on a larger scale than the small-boat fishermen. The fishermen found occasional work with the planters, who outfitted schooners for the spring seal hunt and the Labrador fishery. Their business supported the shipyards. The truck system still defined the relationship between fisherman and merchant, the planter providing an economic buffer between the two.

Despite the flagging fishery, survival skills were well honed, and even in this dim decade all was not doom and gloom. The end of the fishing season when the accounts - no matter how meagre - were settled up was a time for looking ahead. The fishermen pulled up their boats, put away their gear, and took in their winter supplies. Soon it was Christmas Eve, time to set the Yule log ablaze and fire off the muzzle-loaders to mark the beginning of the festive season. No one worked during the 12 days of Christmas. It was a time to let go, to let loose with laughter and gaiety in the crowded kitchens, spinning yarns and making merry with the music and song of the Old Country. The ancient practice of mummering, or jannying, outlawed in 1862, was still part of the celebration, as adults with veiled faces, dressed out-landishly in clothes of the opposite sex, partied from house to house around the harbour. Beware, said the law, any person found dressed as a mummer was subject to arrest and a fine not exceeding 20 shillings. But who cared? In this case the law was lightly applied; at Christmastime, outport peace officers might be every bit as celebratory as the mummers themselves.

There was more than one reason to celebrate that Christmas of 1864. Important people had been around the summer before, talking big plans for Heart's Content – Captain Orlebar of the Royal Navy and that tall, edgy American Cyrus Field. He was spotted going about pick-ing up things like seashells and dead birds, for the Harvard Museum they said, but that was not the real reason he was there. The word was that next summer he was going to send the largest ship in the world, the *Great Eastern*, to lay another cable across the Atlantic and bring it ashore at Heart's Content. Alexander Mackay of the telegraph com-pany was out from St. John's in the fall building a telegraph line from Carbonear, connecting Heart's Content to the trans-island telegraph and on to the mainland of North America. By all indications, there were high times ahead. The people could scarcely imagine what was in store.

Chapter 3

"And there was no more sea"

In June of 1865, Charles W. Lundy, former troubleshooter for the 1858 cable, arrived in Heart's Content to make preparations for the cable landing. At the time, my great-grandfather James Legge was building a two-storey house on the Legge plantation overlooking the south side of the harbour. Lundy bought it partly finished and put a crew to work under James H. Moore, a clever, young jack of all trades, turning it into a telegraph house. Separate sections were prepared for the Anglo-American cable operators and the telegraphers working the landline for the New York, Newfoundland and London Telegraph Company. The men fitted up a room with papered walls and carpeted floors for the cable operators on the first floor, and a stonecutter from St. John's installed two large columns to support the sensitive mirror galvanometers. The telegraph office went in upstairs. Messages coming in on the cable would be written out and passed to the telegraph section for sending overland, the procedure reversed for messages coming from the westward. As these preparations were underway, the telegraph company was finishing the line to Carbonear, connecting to the trans-island service.

On the other side of the ocean, the *Great Eastern* steamed into position off Valentia, Ireland, the cable coiled in her giant storage tanks. On July 22 the eastern end of the cable went ashore at a small sandy beach on the desolate coast of Foilhummerum Bay. Hundreds thronged in for a view of the ship, pitching their tents and canopies in the fields above the looming cliffs where a carnival atmosphere soon prevailed. The sound of the fiddle and pipes wafted through the campground, and young colleens danced the jig as the whiskey jug was passed around. The steamer *Caroline* brought in the heavily armoured shore section of the cable, passing it to the beach over a string of small boats rafted together. The crowd pitched in and helped haul it up the cliff to the telegraph house. No one got to see the *Great Eastern*, anchored far offshore. Early the next morning her engines rumbled to life, and with a small flotilla of supporting vessels she set course for Newfoundland with the slender ocean cable, about the size of a man's finger, snaking out over her stern.

At her destination excitement charged the air. The July 18 *St. John's Daily News* noted, "all the town appear to be preparing for a stampede

Heart's Content in 1865. Note the telegraph line leading to James Legge's house (with the flagpole under the right-hand corner of the church). Toward the water from the church is the Underhay plantation. Around the bend to this side are the premises of Elias Warren. The two wharves to the right of centre are the Hopkins premises. *From Frank Leslie's Illustrated Newspaper, September 9, 1865.*

to the precincts of Heart's Content." Chancey and Heath, proprietors of a St. John's bakery shop, were advertising refreshments, board and sleeping apartments to those wishing to witness the arrival of the *Great Eastern*. By the beginning of August, when word came that she was on her way, Heart's Content was crammed with reporters, illustrators, well-wishers and curiosity seekers. Accommodations were at a premium. Every available house was in use, as were a good many tents, and even a few haylofts and box carts. Enterprising publicans from Harbour Grace and Carbonear had managed to secure two houses as temporary taverns, and were doing a rushing business in spruce beer, ginger beer, brandy and the local favourite "callibogus," a blend of spruce beer and rum. Schoolmaster William Thompson opened the schoolhouse in the middle of summer to keep the children out of harm's way.

So it went for weeks, as they watched and waited for the telegraph fleet. The local press kept a running commentary of news – or lack of it: (July 29 *"Great Eastern* at Valentia July 19"; August 2 "will arrive about the latter part of this week"; August 5 "confirmed the *Great Eastern* sailed"; August 8 "Where is the *Great Eastern?*"; August 11 "very unlikely now that the *Great Eastern* is coming").[1] On board the *Great Eastern*, in fact, the voyage was going badly. Three times the cable had to be hauled back on board and faulty sections repaired. The third time, 600 miles out from Newfoundland, it broke. All efforts to grapple it from the bottom failed, and there was no choice but to end the expedition and return to England. The crowd at Heart's Content packed up and returned to St. John's "deeply disgusted and disappointed."[2]

Reporters of the international press, robbed of a story, put together whatever background copy they could for an early portrayal of this little known place. The *New York Herald* gave a pleasant overview, noting especially that "a finer type of people physically than the Newfoundlanders, bred and born, are not easily to be met with. They are healthy, good looking and splendidly developed."[3] But in keeping with the climate of the times, which lauded progress above all, the depiction of life in an out-of-the-way harbour like Heart's Content was generally not flattering. In addition, the sting of poverty drove people to make the most of their well-cut visitors, as noted by the *New York Times*:

> In the first place there are no buildings of note; in the second place there are no people of any consequence. Nothing in or of itself suggested its name nor secured its present prominence. The bay has done all that will hereafter make the name of the place famous…Civilized men, with garments of modern cut, unsoiled and whole, are to these ingenuous people pregnant with curiosity. No man appears upon the narrow street from abroad without being surrounded and accompanied to his place of destination by a throng of men, women and children…Hotels are unknown; boarding houses, properly so-called, do not

The Telegraph House. *From the Illustrated London News, September 8, 1866.*

exist; *ergo*, the honest inhabitants, seeing the great influx of people who need hotels and boarding-houses, have resolved themselves into a guard of swindlers...These landlords and landladies are bad enough and grasping enough in all conscience; they furnish small rooms at big prices; they spread long tables with slim bills of fare; they complain of the difficulty of obtaining food but charge as though they not only obtained but furnished it...Should success attend the present enterprise – should the laid cable be enabled to do its duty – this place will become one of the curiosities of the hemisphere. It cannot fail to grow and become a great resort. As the seat of fashionable society during the summer months it would be without a rival.[4]

A touch overblown perhaps – Heart's Content was not about to challenge Cape Cod or the French Riviera as a seat of fashionable society, though once the cable came it would attract its share of the Newfoundland tourist trade.

In England, the cable adventurers regrouped. Success had been close enough for Cyrus Field to forestall any opposition. In fact, the cable and the paying-out machinery had worked admirably – the problem was with the grappling equipment. Arrangements were immediately begun for a new expedition the following year. The company directors were so upbeat that they approved a two-pronged strategy to lay a new cable and to raise the one just lost, bringing two lines into service at the same time. Atlantic Telegraph had issued all its allowable shares, so to raise additional capital they chartered the Anglo-American Telegraph Company. Its shares were quickly subscribed.   Through it all, Cyrus Field held everything together, racing around on both sides of the Atlantic tending to the new financing, the refitting of the *Great Eastern*, improvements to the new cable, and the hundreds of details necessary to keep the project afloat. This time, it would all pay off.

On a foggy, rainy July 13, 1866, the shore section of the cable was hoisted aboard the *Great Eastern* from Valentia's Foilhummerum Bay. The splice to the ocean cable was made, and, accompanied by three British escorts (the HMS *Terrible*, the *Albany* and the *Medway*), the great ship set sail once again for Newfoundland. Along with the crew and passengers she carried an assortment of electricians, engineers, telegraph operators and sundry others involved in the cable venture. The ship was under the command of Scottish-born Captain James Anderson. A tall, dignified man of few words (and an amateur magician), Anderson was one of the ablest senior officers in Britain, seconded from the Cunard Line for the cable-laying voyages. Cyrus Field was on hand, his commitment to the project unshakable, and around him were gathered some of the best minds in cable laying and construction.   Samuel Canning, the Chief Engineer of Anglo-American, assisted by Henry Clifford, had been with Field since the first expedition in the Cabot Strait in 1855. Willoughby Smith, intimately connected with cabling and telegraphy since 1849, was the Chief Electrician.   Fidgety and distracted, the electrical genius William Thomson was on board. Among the other principals were John C. Deane, corporate secretary of Anglo-American, and Daniel Gooch, part owner of the *Great Eastern* and a company director.

The ephemeral success of 1858 and the failure of 1865 put a sombre mood to the voyage, but this time they had no reason to worry. Lessons from the previous attempts had been well learned, and apart from a quickly corrected problem with one twisted section of cable, the operation went like clockwork.   Soon after their departure from Valentia, fair weather set in and stayed with them until they neared Newfoundland.   Late in the evening of July 26, surrounded by "a mas-

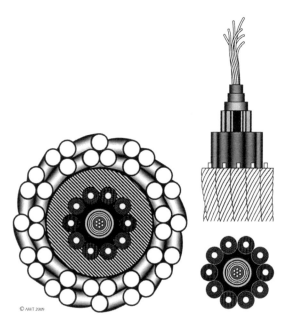

© AWT 2009

The 1865-66 cable, a seven-wire core protected by four layers of insulation, wrapped in tarred hemp, and surrounded by ten stranded iron wires wound in impregnated hemp. The heavy shore end had added insulation and stranded wire protection.

sive curtain of fog"[5] the *Great Eastern* and her convoy steamed slowly into Trinity Bay.

After the no-show of 1865 the reception was restrained, but Heart's Content was again ready and waiting. The reporters were back, the stone columns were dusted off, and a welcoming committee was in place, including Surveyor General J.H. Warren representing the Prime Minister of Newfoundland, and John C. Toussaint, the French Consular Agent and *bon vivant* hotelier from St. John's. People had been drifting into town all through July, again drawn as much by the *Great Eastern* as the cable landing. Anticipation grew as a flotilla of vessels gathered in the harbour – the HMS *Royalist* and *Galatea*, the survey ship *Margaretta* S*tevenson* and five coal ships from Wales sent ahead to refuel the giant cable ship. All around, the atmosphere was festive. The British and American flags flew from the church and the telegraph station. The sale of liquor was brisk.

Now cast your thoughts back to Friday, July 27, 1866 and watch as the events of that historic day unfold:[6]

4:00 a.m. The sound of gunfire on the *Great Eastern* brings Daniel Gooch on deck, but there is no cause for alarm. The HMS *Niger* has begun piloting the cable ship through the fog toward Heart's Content harbour, marking her position with a periodic gun blast.

6:00 a.m. The thick, grey fog enveloping Trinity Bay begins to abate a little. Paying no heed to history in the making, the fishermen are already on the water busily working their handlines. At Freshwater, four miles past Heart's Content, some of them sight the *Albany* looming up in the fog, way off course for the harbour where she must clear an anchorage for the *Great Eastern*. The fishermen direct her to the harbour entrance.

7:30 a.m. The *Great Eastern*, or the "Big Eastern" as the locals call her, steams slowly past New Perlican three miles short of Heart's Content. A cry goes up in the village and people run to find a vantage point to watch her huge hulk gliding by through the veil of fog.

8:00 a.m. With the fog lifting, the *Great Eastern* is just off Heart's Content. The *Albany* steams into the harbour to position a boat with a red flag as a marker for Captain Anderson's anchorage. At the same time, the *Margaretta Stevenson* is running out to meet the giant ship, whose channel into the harbour is laid out with a series of markers. The *Great Eastern* fires a salute and three cheers go up from the crew. The cheers are answered by a crowd of 120, mostly young people, assembled at the harbour entrance on Northern Point. Boats begin to put off from shore, rowing out to meet the fleet.

9:00 a.m. A small boat brings Cyrus Field ashore to see that all is ready for the cable. For him, it is yet another crisis when he finds out from Alexander Mackay that the cable across the Cabot Strait has gone down, breaking contact with the rest of North America. He immediately wires St. John's, chartering the *Bloodhound* to make repairs and the *Dauntless* to ferry messages across the Strait until the cable becomes operational.

10:30 a.m. Just outside the harbour, two guns from the *Great Eastern* announce that the cable is cut. The end of the ocean cable is lowered over her stern and moved to the *Medway* to be spliced to the shore section.

The *Great Eastern* at Heart's Content. *Courtesy PANL.*

11:00 a.m. Using her side paddles, the *Great Eastern* pivots slowly on her centre, a manoeuvre that astonishes the crowd of onlookers. Then, under blue skies and bright sunshine, and with scarcely a ripple on the water, she glides to her berth on the northeast side of the harbour. Boats cluster around bringing visitors from shore, curious for an up-close view of the most magnificent ship afloat.

12 noon. The *Medway* steams slowly into the harbour paying out the shore section of the cable, dropping anchor a hundred yards from the telegraph house.

2:00 p.m. From the *Medway*, the shore end is coiled in a large flat-bottomed paddleboat brought along especially for the purpose and taken toward the beach. There is now a long delay when it is discovered that no one can point out the actual landing site. Alexander Mackay says it is none of his business and retires to the telegraph office to wait things out. Eventually, Daniel Gooch and Samuel Canning come ashore and select a landing place at Elias Warren's premises. Men set to work digging a trench for the cable across the road and up to the telegraph office.

Finally, all is ready. Fifty sailors from the *Terrible* have been idling about on the beach, each wanting to be the first to bring the cable in.

As the landing craft approaches, they all rush into the water. Someone breaks a bottle of champagne on the end of the cable as it leaves the boat, and the sailors begin dragging the line ashore "hugging it in their brawny arms as if it were a shipwrecked child whom they had rescued from the dangers of the sea."[7] There is the greatest of cheering and shouting from the spectators. Mrs. John Bemister of Harbour Grace, caught up in the excitement, pushes her way to the beach and to the crowd's delight grabs hold of the cable along with the sailors, dragging it to the shore. The minute the cable touches land a signal is given and all the ships in the harbour fire a salute, the boom reverberating around the hills.

4:00 p.m. The cable reaches the telegraph house amid another burst of delirium. Daniel Gooch was astounded: "The old cable hands seemed as though they could eat the end; one man actually put it into his mouth and sucked it. They held it up and danced round it, cheering at the top of their voices."[8] (Sucking on the cable is not as deviant as it might sound; apparently it was not unusual for electricians to relish the acidic "taste" of a telegraphic current.) The cable is connected to the instruments, and Gooch sends the first message to Valentia that the landing is accomplished. Clear signals are exchanged between the two stations.

5:30 p.m. Cyrus Field, the ships' officers and others proceed to the church for a Thanksgiving Service conducted by George Gardner, who delivers an excellent sermon on the text "And there was no more sea." His sister Emma from Harbour Grace provides the music on the church's small pump organ.

6:30 p.m. After church, the party returns to the telegraph house. The seamen and officers then set off to their ships for dinner and further celebration. On shore, the merrymaking continues into the night and includes a display of fireworks, which apparently is disappointing: one observer finds them "very poor and very scanty, a few rockets only.[9]

As in 1858, there was widespread jubilation on the news that the cable had reached Heart's Content. In St. John's, church bells pealed, bands marched, crowds filled the streets and ships were decked out with flags and bunting. All business came to a halt. Music and gunfire were heard

Landing the cable at Heart's Content, July 27, 1866.
From a watercolour by Robert Dudley. Courtesy Peter Winkworth Collection, Library and Archives Canada.

well into the evening as people partied in the streets under a drenching downpour of rain.

The next few days in Heart's Content saw a steady stream of sightseers boarding the *Great Eastern*. John Deane, secretary of Anglo-American, wrote, "The velvet-covered sofas in the ladies' saloon found a succession of occupants in the persons of the fair daughters of Heart's Content."[10] One of the visitors that caught Deane's attention was a blind girl, later identified as Mary Piercey of Scilly Cove, who was led around the ship by her young brother. "It was touching to see the radiant smile on that poor girl's face as she listened to the boy, who told her of the wonders he saw."[11]

The festivities carried on through the week. On Monday, July 30, Captain Anderson entertained all the officers of the fleet on board the *Great Eastern*, with much glad-handing, back-patting and speech-making. On Thursday, loaded into carriages, they all trundled across the Barrens to Harbour Grace and a 100-guest society ball hosted by Mr. and Mrs. T.H. Ridley in a special tent splendidly decorated for the occasion. Deane noted the "opportunity afforded them by their fair hostess of seeing that Newfoundland can hold its own with any other part of the world in the beauty of its women."[12] On Saturday, the officers of the *Great Eastern* returned the favour when some of the ladies from the

Ridley soiree were invited to dine on board. They "improvised a dance in the evening"[13] and a dozen or so consented to stay the night. Internationally, the cable landing was the news of the day, headlining the papers of Europe and North America, and for the second year in a row placed Newfoundland squarely in the eyes of the world. For the down-to-earth folk of Heart's Content, wary of strangers to begin with, the attention was a sobering experience. They may have been uninformed of the niceties of modern ways, but as a reporter for the *Boston Journal* found out, they did not take kindly to the previous year's description as a "guard of swindlers" living in a place of no merit:

> It seems that the correspondents of the New York press, on their previous visits, had amused themselves with sketching the life and character of the people; and their essays, however amusing they may have been in the States, were read with genuine indignation in the Island by the more ignorant inhabitants. It was their first test of the bitters of civilization…The simple fishers were as furious with the work of the editors as they were amazed at the works of the electricians.

> A gentleman applied to the wife of a 'planter' for board for the two of us. We represented leading journals. The old lady was willing to accommodate, but when she was told that we were correspondents, she declared that she would have 'nothing to do with any of us!' And she didn't.[14]

The stories continued to spin out, the Victorian bias at full throttle, the cultural gap between visitor and native yawning ever wider. A writer for *Chambers' Journal*, arriving on the *Great Eastern*, sniffed:

> Heart's Content is not what would be called an interesting place…The village itself consists of a wooden church, and about a hundred wooden houses, all built in a most unpretending style of architecture…The commerce of the place consists of codfish, which are dried in the sun, and dispense an aroma that is anything but nice.[15]

Of course the smell of salt codfish drying in the sun, the fruits of a profitable voyage, was likely as pleasant to a Heart's Content fisherman as it was malodorous to a Londoner. Indeed, the Heart's Content man might have found the smells of London, trying at the time to cope with the sewage of three million people, more than a little offensive to him. The *Boston Journal* correspondent, once he found someone to take him in, was only slightly more charitable:

> The houses are all old and shabby, and built without regard to taste. Windows seem to be put in with exclusive reference to inside use. The people are all poor fishers, with two or three exceptions. These are the small class of "planters" – a sort of agents for the great merchants, who contract with the fishermen for their services, and act as middlemen in other ways. They are not rich, but they are better off than the fishermen. These are practically serfs. Not the whip but the ledger keeps them constantly in the merchant's debt and power.
>
> There is a great difference in them. They are all poor and ignorant and superstitious; but some of their houses are models of neatness, while others are exactly the reverse. They have all the big old chimney corners, with the woodfire on the hearth, and the upright highway overhead through which the smoke escapes – of which we read so much in descriptions of the bygone times, but which we never see now in the United States. The crook hangs down and supports the kettles as they did in the revolutionary days at home. These chimney corners are really little rooms with benches to sit on at both sides of the fire.[16]

The locals were understandably miffed at the reports depicting their home as a backward, grasping and smelly place. They may well have wondered why the skills of fishing and shipbuilding, indeed the fortitude needed to maintain any kind of civilized existence here, went unnoticed. Nor did anyone read of the powerful mutual-support ethic typical of a Newfoundland outport and recently formalized in the Heart's Content Fishermen's Society.

There was scant recognition of the tightly knit, resilient culture that had evolved "hidden away behind the fogs."

The hard-pressed representative of the *Boston Journal* did find some distinctiveness worthy of note:

> The people of the Colony are nearly all either West of England or Irish, with just Scotch enough to keep up a good supply of pure Highland whisky. Among the fishermen you hear the uncouth phrases of the "West Country" commonly mingled with Irish idiom. The poorest class have a distinct and peculiar dialect, therefore neither British nor Yankee, but born of the spongy soil of Newfoundland. I hope that some writer will arise among them to preserve it to literature and to paint their mode of life and thought ere they pass away forever before the advance of education.[17]

No fear of that, as witnessed by the blossoming of cultural self-awareness that has swept Newfoundland in the last half century.

But back to the business of the cable. On August 9, following an overnight visit by the governor of the colony, Anthony Musgrave, the *Great Eastern* left Heart's Content to recover the line abandoned in 1865. After three and a half weeks of meticulous work with the *Albany* and the *Terrible,* the cable was retrieved and spliced to the 600-mile length left over from the year before. At Valentia, an operator who had spent the past year monitoring the condition of the lost cable saw his receiving instrument suddenly spring to life with a message from the *Great Eastern.* He telegraphed back that all was in order. On the ship, Cyrus Field went to his cabin and locked the door. "I could no longer restrain my tears," he later wrote, "crying like a child, and full of gratitude to God that I had been permitted to live to witness the recovery of the cable we had lost from the *Great Eastern* just thirteen months previous."[18]

On September 8, the *Great Eastern* landed the second cable at Heart's Content, to a second jubilant reception, described by Henry Field:

> As the ships came up the harbour it was covered with boats, and all were wild with excitement; and when the big shore-end was got out of the *Medway* and dragged to land, the sailors hugged it and almost kissed it in

their extravagance of joy; and no sooner was it safely landed than they seized Mr. Field, Mr. Canning and Mr. Clifford in their arms, and raised them over their heads, while the crowd cheered with tumultuous enthusiasm.[19]

It was a double victory: two functioning cables across the Atlantic. By this time Alexander Mackay had also replaced the Cape Breton cable, giving Anglo-American an exclusive link in a communication chain extending from London to New York. For the first time, the weary cable investors stood to earn a return. The shares of Anglo-American, trading at a discount prior to the cable landing, were now at a premium of 25%.

The second cable safe on shore, the *Great Eastern* began preparations to depart Heart's Content. With the mission that had eluded them so many times finally concluded, the cable adventurers found their elation tinged with nostalgia. Even the hard-nosed businessman Daniel Gooch was wistful. "Heart's Content looked quite homely to me today," he wrote. "We sail tomorrow, and I suppose I will then take my last look at it. Well, I will never forget it."[20] Leaving the ship for the last time, Cyrus Field clasped the hand of Captain Anderson in an emotional farewell. "Give him three cheers!" shouted the normally taciturn Scotsman to his crew. "And now three more for his family!"[21] As darkness fell on the evening of September 9, the *Great Eastern* fired four guns and glided out of the harbour, bound for England.

When they reached home, the leaders of the expedition, including James Anderson, Samuel Canning and William Thomson, were honoured with knighthoods, and Daniel Gooch became a baronet. The success of Thomson's inventions would make him a wealthy man, allowing him the extravagance of a private yacht, a luxury shared by few academics, even knighted ones. He later became Lord Kelvin, his name immortalized on the scientific scale of absolute temperature.

Cyrus Field returned to New York to another round of banquets, toasts and public recognition. As an American citizen, he was not eligible for a knighthood, but the US Congress issued a special medal in his honour. With all his wealth poured into the dream of an Atlantic cable, he made a second fortune for bringing it all together. He invested in other businesses and travelled the world. He backed a Pacific cable to Asia and Australia, and helped finance the building of an elevated railroad system in New York City, but his later years were not happy. In the

1880s he suffered a series of financial setbacks, lost heavily in the stock market and saw his fortune wiped out. He died on July 12, 1892, at the age of 73. Carried home and laid to rest in Stockbridge, his epitaph reads simply: "Cyrus West Field – To whose courage, energy and perseverance the world owes the Atlantic telegraph."

Missing from the crowd who witnessed the cable landing was Frederic Gisborne. After a try at mineral exploration in Newfoundland and the Maritime provinces, he went back to England to live out the 1860s. There he patented a series of inventions in telegraphy and navigation but was swindled out of any financial success. He returned to Canada in 1869 to oversee developments in the mining of coal and gold in Nova Scotia, but both projects failed. Ten years later he became superintendent of the Canadian telegraph service, where he remained until his death in Ottawa on August 30, 1892, just weeks after Cyrus Field. Shut out of the original circle of the New York, Newfoundland and London Telegraph Company, Gisborne, as it happened, outlived them all.

Chapter 4

Communications Outpost

Landing the cable was one thing. Keeping it working was another. After the *Great Eastern* departed Heart's Content and the excitement had died down, the employees of Anglo-American and the New York, Newfoundland and London Telegraph Company settled into the business of providing a reliable trans-ocean telegraph service. The station was on the cutting edge of communication, but with the technology still in its infancy, there were more than a few challenges to overcome.[1]

Considering all the planning and preparation that went into laying the cable, arrangements to set up facilities at Heart's Content were surprisingly lax. James Legge's house, secured for an office in 1865, was not at all suitable, and the company immediately needed more space. Cyrus Field swung into action, offering Elias Warren the unheard-of sum of $2,000 for his two-acre plantation, a figure the veteran businessman was quick to accept.[2] Warren's house provided a temporary office plus living quarters for some of the staff. The station relocated there on September 8. A second staff house went up, and the company engaged the premiere building contractors of St. John's, brothers John & James T. Southcott, to begin work on an office building. Eventually, James Legge got his house back.

The new office, a modest wood-frame affair, was ready by mid-November. Anglo-American (known locally as the "English company") moved into the north end of the building, and the New York, Newfoundland and London Telegraph Company (the "American company") occupied the south end. Messages passed back and forth between the cable and land sides through a partition with a slide pane. Different technologies demanded the physical separation of the cable and landlines. The familiar key and sounder used in land telegraphy was not adaptable for cable reception. Cable operators telegraphed out with a double key, but Thomson's mirror galvanometer, set up on a vibration-free base in a darkened room, was at the heart of operations as the receiving instrument. The operator read the cable messages to an assistant at a rate of about eight words per minute, much slower than the 25-30 words per minute typical of land telegraphy.

The initial rate charged on the cable was very expensive: £1 per

The Cable Station c.1869.

word with a minimum of £20 per message. Put in perspective, an operator's annual wage at the time was in the range of £200. The pricing restricted use of the service to government, big business and the very wealthy, but it generated huge income. Between July 27 and August 31, 1866, 1,104 messages passed through Heart's Content, bringing in close to £32,000.[3] In November, the minimum tariff was reduced to £10, and it continued to drop over the years as other companies entered the business. But at the outset the Atlantic cable earned substantial revenues - £30,000 or more per month was not uncommon.

Opening up communication between the continents had an immediate impact on both sides of the Atlantic. Newspapers were of course heavy users of the service, their readers savouring the novelty of the latest news headlines from the other side of the ocean. Business and commerce benefited in other ways. With commodity quotes available daily between New York and London, prices normalized on the two markets. No longer could a shortage of cotton, say, in Europe drive up the price if a ready supply was available in North America. Shipping improved as communication allowed precise scheduling of voyages. And with observations available from both sides of the ocean, weather forecasting became more reliable.

Navigation also improved. Even before the cable landed, arrangements were already in place to use it to standardize positions of longitude. George W. Dean of the United States Coast Survey was among

Ezra Weedon (1839-1884).
Courtesy Department of Tourism, Culture and Recreation, Provincial Historic Sites Branch

the crowd at Heart's Content waiting for the *Great Eastern.* He and his assistant Edward Goodfellow set up a small observatory across the road from the cable office, and during the crisp fall nights of 1866 calibrated astronomical readings with observations at Valentia and Calais, Maine, producing the first direct measurements of longitude between Europe and North America.[4]

These advances were made despite the fact that in the beginning the cable service was far from reliable. The minute sensitivity of the mirror galvanometer, the key to cable reception, made it extremely susceptible to outside interference. The earth's magnetic currents, lightning, the aurora borealis, and other unexplained phenomena sent the spot of light on the instrument into wild and rapid gyrations. Bad weather on both sides of the Atlantic played havoc with the landlines as well, which were frequently downed by rain, wind, snow and lightning. The cables were also prone to damage by ships' anchors and icebergs. In 1870, icebergs grounded on the '66 cable on three separate occasions. Before repairs could be completed, the '65 cable went down, leaving Heart's Content with no service at all for seven months. During this time, messages were routed through St. Pierre, where La Société du Cable Transatlantique Française had installed a cable service the year before. At the time, the French company was the only competition for Anglo-American on the transatlantic route, and that did not last long. Anglo bought them out in 1873.

At Heart's Content, there was a lot of fiddling with the receiving instrument in an effort to improve its reliability, with various placements of the lamp, scale and galvanometer attempted to produce more dependable readings. Operators sat in front of the apparatus hour after hour, tinkering with the mirror and adjusting the suspension fibres. They also experimented endlessly with the load on the cables, varying the amount of battery power and resistance in the circuits, trying the cables alternately and in combination. The men were working in uncharted waters, learning as they went, gradually bringing long-distance cabling to a rapid, reliable mode of communication.

The Anglo-American employees who arrived at Heart's Content on the *Great Eastern* were well versed in the business of cable telegraphy.

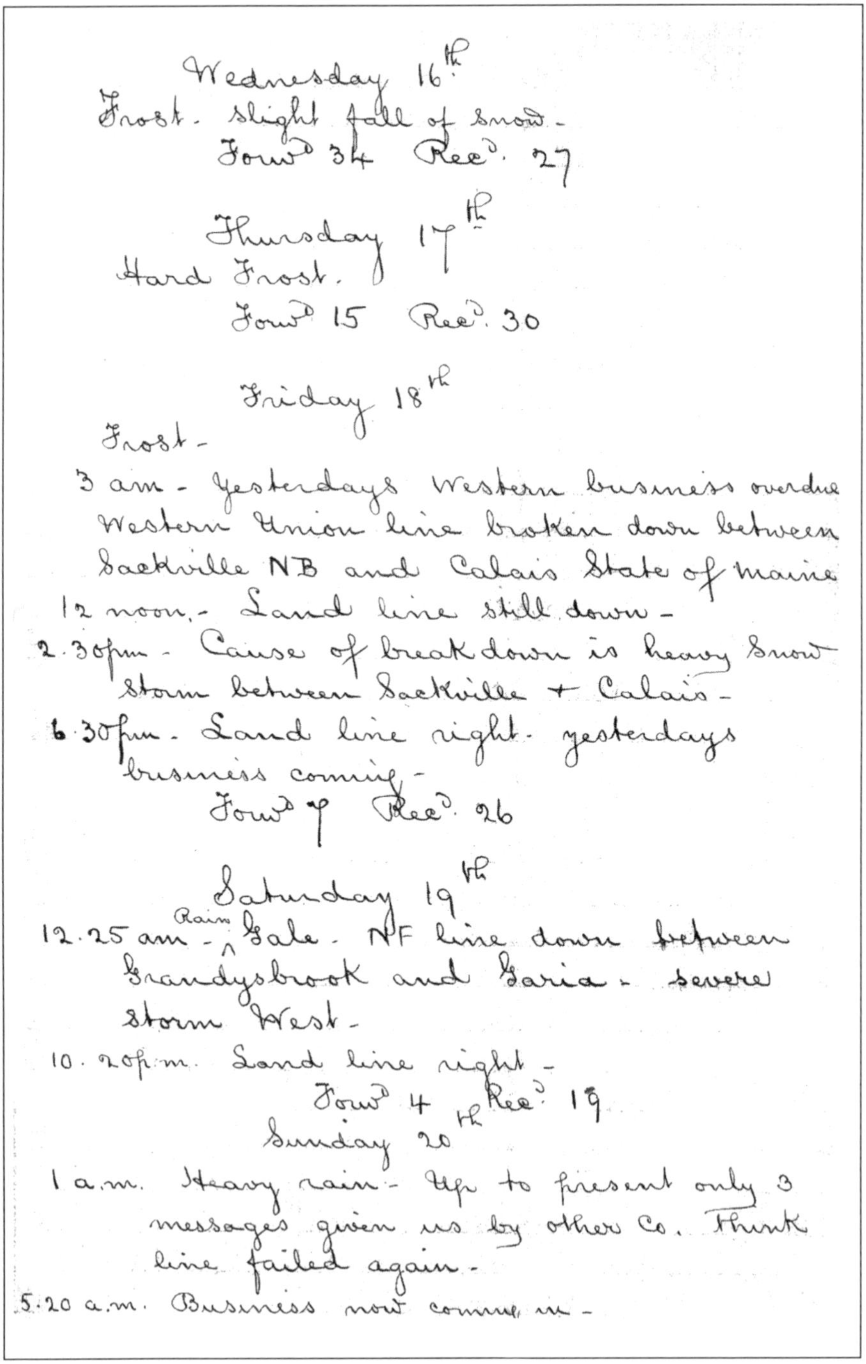

Wednesday 16th
Frost. slight fall of snow -
Tour 34   Rec. 27

Thursday 17th
Hard Frost.
Tour 15   Rec. 30

Friday 18th
Frost -
3 am - yesterdays Western business overdue
Western Union line broken down between
Sackville NB and Calais State of maine
12 noon, - Land line still down -
2.30pm - Cause of break down is heavy Snow
Storm between Sackville + Calais -
6.30pm - Land line right - yesterdays
business coming -
Tour 9   Rec. 26

Saturday 19th
12.25 am - Rain - Gale - NF line down between
Brandysbrook and Baria - severe
Storm West -
10.20pm - Land line right -
Tour 4   Rec. 19
Sunday 20th
1 a.m. Heavy rain - Up to present only 3
messages given us by other Co. Think
line failed again -
5.20 a.m. Business now coming in -

Excerpt from the Anglo-American daily journal, Heart's Content, January 1867.

Charles W. Lundy, the first superintendent, supervised the operation of the station, assisted by Richard Collett as traffic superintendent and Ezra Weedon as clerk in charge. The operators who started work on July 28, 1866, were Frank Perry, George Unicume, Charles Trippe and William Woodcock, all single men from England. Perry, the senior man, thoughtful and steady, and Trippe, an easygoing fellow, had both worked as assistants to William Thomson on the cable-laying voyage. Woodcock was a jumpy sort, competent and reliable but deemed too nervous

William Dickenson (1841-1911).
Courtesy Dennis O'Brien.

to make a first-class operator. Unicume, a quiet and frail 19-year-old had a kindly disposition, friendly to all. Collett discovered that he had only five operators to fill a schedule needing a complement of six, so on the spot hired John Sullivan, a devil-may-care Irishman who had taken passage on the *Great Eastern* en route to the United States. William Toussaint, a sometime hotelier and baker from Harbour Grace and son of J.C. Toussaint, the French Consular Agent, came on as a recording clerk but ill health forced his resignation within the year.

Lundy and Collett returned to England before the end of 1866, where Collett became Anglo's general manager, and 27-year-old Ezra Weedon took over as superintendent. A tiny man (he stood only 4 ft. 6 inches tall)[5], Weedon came from the village of Dinton in Buckinghamshire, the illegitimate son of a lacemaker. He was bright, intense and cocky, with an underlying touchiness, but his generous heart and sense of fair play quickly earned him the respect of the staff. With Weedon as superintendent, Frank Perry became senior clerk, and in November James Bartlett joined the staff from London. The other Englishmen included William Dickenson, a combination mechanic and electrician (a "mechanician" in cable parlance) who had also worked as electrician on the *Great Eastern*. George Charlton, experienced in cable construction and maintenance, was brought over to look after the outside work.[6]

Dickenson attracted attention in communication circles within a few months of starting at the station. With Wildman Whitehouse removed from the controls, the submarine cables were operating on very low battery power – of the order of 10 volts. Latimer Clarke, a telegraph electrician in England, was curious to find out just how low he could take the voltage and still drive a signal. At Valentia he concocted a tiny bat·ery using sulphuric acid in a lady's thimble, and one quiet Sunday morning in September 1866 asked the Heart's Content station to monitor the spare cable. Amazingly, signals powered by the thimble batte·y came through. A few Sundays later Valentia was asked to monitor the spare line, and they reported reception, though very weak. Dickenson had managed to one-up Clarke's experiment by transmitting signals with a tiny battery made from a percussion gun cap.[7] Family tradition has it that the gun cap battery went on display at the Smithsonian Institute. During his time in Heart's Content, Dickenson patented a number of enhancements to the service, including an improved key and sounder and a vibrating apparatus used to stabilize reception on Thomson's recorder. He was awarded a bronze medal from Edward VII, then Prince of Wales, for his contributions to electrical science.[8]

At the outset, security at the station was high on the minds of the staff. It was a time when the whole of British North America was on edge from the threat of attack by the Fenians, a militant Irish movement active in the United States that had made a few highly publicized sorties across the Canadian border. In the spring of 1866, rumours of a Fenian gunboat lying offshore sent St. John's into widespread panic.[9] As the *Great Eastern* and her convoy were preparing to depart Heart's Content on September 9, there were reports of a plot to sabotage the cable operation, and HMS *Lily* was detained on guard. In November a gunboat was assigned to protect the cables off the Irish coast. Further concern about security was expressed by Weedon to Anglo secretary John Deane on December 7:

> I shall be glad if you will consider the expediency of firearms being supplied to Newfoundland staff – it is possible that they may only be used as a source of amusement, but I think while Fenianism is so rife and this place so entirely open to them, that we should use every precaution in case of anything happening.[10]

Whether firearms were supplied or not made no difference. The Fenians made no attempt to disrupt cable operations.

The newcomers worked away at the station while the rest of Heart's Content worked at adjusting to their presence. In a town that occu-

pied itself with the cod fishery, sealing and shipbuilding, cable operators were in a class of their own. The gap was made that much wider
by the fact that no Heart's Content men, even those with a degree of
literacy, were hired to work there. Anglo-American preferred cable
hands from England, and the New York, Newfoundland and London
Telegraph Company brought in their own experienced operators
from the mainland and places like St. John's, Brigus and Harbour
Grace. It was almost a decade before John Ollerhead, stepson of John
Sullivan, became the first local man to join the staff. However, the
cable brought spin-off demands for labour and services that benefited
the entire community. Buildings went up, the staff hired domestic servants, and odd jobs came along, all of it paid for in hard currency.
The employees themselves were paid in cash, shipped in monthly
from St. John's. It circulated around to the merchants and planters,
and some of it trickled down to the hard-pressed fishing families.

The station added a whole new layer to the social and cultural life of
the community. Before 1866, the people of standing were the clergy,
the schoolteacher, the magistrate and a few merchants and planters.
At the time of the cable landing George Gardner, the hard-working
clergyman and founder of the Fishermen's Society, was the leading
citizen. Now suddenly there was a new group, highly paid, well educated and worldly, most of them from outside the country with a
Victorian predisposition toward class.

North America's egalitarian society of today is far removed from the
rigid class structure that dominated life in Victorian England. Social
class was of overriding importance, and it revealed itself in a number
of ways: in manners, speech, clothing, education, and values. Each
class had its own rules of behaviour and people were expected to con-
form to them. Society frowned upon anyone behaving like someone
from a class above – or below – one's own. Needless to say, movement
of individuals between classes was not a common occurrence.

In Heart's Content the newcomers stood apart from the locals in
their tailored suits, porkpie and bowler hats, their sophisticated manner and polished speech, and how they chose to amuse themselves.
Back home they were middle-class telegraphers. Here they were elevated (or elevated themselves) to elite status. A well-practised deference to the British on the part of the Newfoundlanders ensured that
they maintained it.

The cable station ran like a quasi-military operation. The men
didn't go to work, they showed up for duty. While employed, they

were said to be "in the service." They ate at the mess, and instead of taking vacation they went on leave. The superintendent's word was law The operators worked eight-hour shifts, in pairs, seven days a week. The work required discipline and strict attention. It was occasionally hectic, usually wearisome, but not hard.

Compared to England, living conditions at Heart's Content were less than ideal. The cable staff roomed in rented homes, the two company houses or in the office building itself. Anglo did its best to provide for their comfort, but the rough-built local houses were draughty and cold. The first year was mild, rather like England. Then came 1867-68, when they were hit with the full force of a Newfoundland winter. For the Englishmen, it was rough going. The snow whipped around the wood frame buildings, piling into 10-foot drifts and blowing through open cracks in the walls. The thermometers sent to Weedon for meteorological observation did not register low enough to track the temperature.[11]

In early February the hazards of winter life in Newfoundland became all too apparent. On Monday, February 3, 1868 with bad weather threatening, a group of 30 impoverished men and boys, their families out of food, set out from Heart's Content to Harbour Grace in search of provisions. That evening on Heart's Content Barrens they were caught in the full fury of a mid-winter storm. With no place to seek shelter, 13 of them froze to death.[12] The disaster drove home the need for a place of refuge on the lonely, desolate stretch of road. The following year Anglo committed £50 toward building a halfway house that was completed, with a government caretaker in place, in 1870.[13]

The cable operators, meanwhile, trying to slog through the winter of 1868, were thoroughly miserable. Weedon informed head office in his precise, rounded script:

> Sickness is becoming very prevalent among the staff – during the past month or 5 weeks all have been attacked more or less, and at the present time I have 2 operators (Perry and Crocker) away ill, and Charlton has been confined to his bed nearly a month. There is no doubt whatever that the sole cause of the sickness is draughts while sitting in the house and during the night when in bed.[14]

In fact, Henry Ring Crocker, recently arrived from Valentia, proved unable to cope at all: "at times his senses seem to fail entirely – another Newfoundland winter would be too much for him."[15] Weedon shipped him back to Ireland.

The station had a desperate need for medical services. The young doctor at Heart's Content, Arthur Buchannan, was an habitual drinker whose wife had deserted him. He spent his time carousing with off-duty staff, and according to Weedon was "fit for nothing."[16] He soon moved to Trinity to live with his mother and sister and died shortly after. With Buchannan gone, the closest physician was in Harbour Grace. The company provided Frank Perry with a medical reference book, and he did his best to attend to the sick until Edward Martin, a graduate of Trinity College, Dublin, arrived in September 1870. Martin was the first in an unbroken line of physicians attached to the station who provided medical service to Heart's Content and other communities nearby, a welcome collateral benefit of the cable.

Work on permanent living quarters for the staff got underway in the spring of 1868, when the Southcott firm broke ground for a block of apartments on the road in front of the office. Designed by a Dublin architect, Cable Terrace was an impressive 2½-storey structure, 210 feet in length, that took a year and a half to complete at a cost of £5,000. It was Newfoundland's most magnificent apartment block outside St. John's. The central section contained bachelor quarters, complete with two mess rooms, a billiard room and library, with each of the two wings providing four seven-room family apartments.

The new building was finished in style. An entire shipload of furnishings came in from England, right down to fine linens and crockery. The company built an icehouse to keep the iceboxes supplied. Weedon happily reported that a long-awaited billiard table was serving its purpose in getting off-duty men out of the office. Anglo made a donation toward books for the library, and Weedon chipped in the small allowance he was receiving for recording the weather. The staff formed the Heart's Content Literary Society, which over time built a collection of some 2,000 volumes, mostly popular fiction of the day, along with technical journals and periodicals. Especially prized was a complete set of the novels of Sir Walter Scott donated by William Thomson and inscribed, "To the superintendent and clerks of the Heart's Content Station, Atlantic Telegraph – W.T. Aug 5, 1866."[17] Down through the years, the library was a unique resource available to the families of staff, but, like the rest of the station, closed to the community at large.

Cable Terrace c.1870. *Courtesy Barbara Hopkins.*

Compared to Valentia, where for the first two years the operators were crammed into a tiny wooden building atop the cliffs of Foilhummerum Bay, five miles from the nearest town, the staff at Heart's Content had little reason to complain. The company justified the preferential treatment accorded them, including higher pay, as compensation for the remote location far removed from their homeland. The discrimination, however, fuelled an early rivalry between the two stations, aggravated by Richard Collett's overbearing disposition and Ezra Weedon's prickly defensiveness. Both men had little patience with what they saw as incompetence on the part of Valentia operators, and Weedon fiercely defended the actions of his own staff against all complaints from James Graves, superintendent at Valentia. An exchange between Collett, still in Newfoundland, and Graves in October 1866 underscores the conflict:

> **Collett**: Attention at your station disgraceful. See it altered. Four messages delayed seventeen minutes before call answered and further twelve minutes before clerk commenced to receive. Send name of clerk on duty.

Graves: When we conferred together it was considered imperatively necessary that good feeling should exist amongst the staff. When I complained of your station you telegraphed Chairman that my message created ill feeling. What can be the effect of yours? George and Mackey were on duty, the former attending fire in kitchen, latter calls of nature in field. "Wait" was given by former till return of latter to write. My staff are competent to do their work and they do it to the best of their ability.[18]

Acrimony between the two stations continued for years, with ill-tempered operators intentionally slowing down transmissions, speeding up when asked to repeat a message and sending offensive remarks over the line. Frank Perry, an old friend of Graves, seemed to be the only one to maintain a civil relationship. They fell into the routine of exchanging greetings in verse at Christmastime, like these genial couplets from Perry in 1879:

> Full thirteen years hath Phoebus' cart gone round
> This icebound shore and Paddy's Emerald ground
> Since each near each in fleshy guise could stand
> And grasp at Christmas time the friendly hand.
> Still are we not much better off than some
> Who no such link enjoy 'twixt them and home
> Through it our hearty greetings are conveyed
> And warmest wishes for "Merry Christmas" made
> Let's hope the festive season may be spent
> Right gladly at VA and Heart's Content.[19]

At the same time, Weedon and the Anglo staff worked smoothly with the operators of the New York, Newfoundland and London Telegraph Company in the other end of the building. Reporting to General Superintendent Alexander Mackay in St. John's, the American company in 1868 had seven men at Heart's Content under superintendent John Waddell: Alexander Saunders, George Carson, Sam Bailey, Edward Moore, Samuel Earle, William Mitchell and John T. Smith.[20] These men worked only the landline. They were not trained to read the mirror galvanometer, nor could they work in International Morse Code, a slightly different version from the American Morse Code of the land telegraph. They could not transfer from the land side to the cable side, and their pay was less. But both groups shared the same social circle. We have a rich record of it from Sam Bailey, the only Newfoundlander on the staff and an inveterate letter-writer who kept up a flood of correspondence with his family in Oderin, Placentia Bay. His letters provide a unique personal glimpse of life at the station in the early years.

Chapter 5

Letters from Sam

Samuel Scott Bailey came to work at Heart's Content in January 1868, while the Anglo staff were struggling through their first Newfoundland winter. Sam grew up in Oderin, a small isolated outport on the west side of Placentia Bay, the second in a family of twelve children. His early schooling, advanced for the time, came from his British-educated father, Nelson Collingwood Bailey, Oderin's first schoolmaster. In 1861, at age 16, Sam landed a job as a linesman and repairman with the New York, Newfoundland and London Telegraph Company on the trans-island telegraph, spending much of his time at

Sam Bailey (1845-1890).
Courtesy Department of Tourism, Culture and Recreation, Provincial Historic Sites Branch.

Long Harbour, Fortune Bay. During the long, lonely hours on the line, he taught himself telegraphy and aspired to an inside job as an operator. Superintendent Alexander Mackay, taken with his diligence, gave him the opportunity he sought at the station in Heart's Content.

On his arrival, just out of the wilds of the South Coast, Sam had a most favourable impression of the place. He informed his mother that the offices were "well fitted up and found in everything," and the staff of both the English and American companies were "all fine smart well-educated men – jovial fellows...we mix a great deal with one another no one thinking himself better than the other."[1] His boss, 40-year-old John Waddell, was "a very nice man" although the bookkeeper John Smith, while clever in his business, was "rather disagreeable as a companion." John Sullivan, half Irish and half Spanish, was the wit of the group, and Sam considered Ezra Weedon as "wonderfully clever and social withal."[2]

Sam's pay was $800 per year, the equivalent of £160.[3] For this he worked a rotating eight-hour shift, with night duty 11 p.m. – 6 a.m. every third week. It was a respectable salary for the day – roughly US $22,500 in today's currency – though below the £175 – £250 received

Staff at the cable station c.1872: A.A. Thompson, E. Moore, S.S. Stentaford, J.T. Collins, C. Newitt, J.T. O'Mara, J. Mitchell, J. Scanlon, A. Courteen, A.R. Martin, J. Bartlett, I.H. Angel, W. Woodcock, Dr. E.N. Martin. *Courtesy Department of Tourism, Culture and Recreation, Provincial Historic Sites Branch.*

by the Anglo men working the cable. The company provided lodging but Sam was responsible for his board, or share of the company mess table, the cost of which he found very expensive. However, the staff all lived "in the best style as regards the inward man – supper every night of the best at 11 or 12 o'clock."[4] The midnight feasts, which coincided with the changeover of duty, began to show on Sam, who went from 230 to 261 pounds within a few years of his arrival.

Liquor flowed freely among the operators, at two local taverns and a small pub provided for their convenience by George Charlton. At Charlton's Pig and Whistle there was no bartender; patrons were on the honour system for settling their tabs. Sam joined in with the crowd when he first arrived, but soon dropped out because of the cost of buying rounds, which was expected of everyone who drank. He was also aware of the risks: "Liquor is ruinous for operators moreso than other professions, especially when you're on night duty."[5]

"This is a beautiful place to live in summer," Sam gushed, "fine roads, good deal of farming going on together with the healthy climate makes it quite agreeable."[6] After the dreary winters, summer could indeed be glorious with soft, sunny days crowned by golden sunsets over Trinity Bay. It was perfect for picnic excursions. Over 30 people turned out for one at Seal Cove, including "all the ladies in the place."[7] Sam befriended two St. John's girls, daughters of businessman Valentine Merchant, whose death the previous year had left them in rather poor circumstances. They kept a small shop near the Main Brook, where Sam often called on them for walks after supper. He thought them "very pretty, well educated & splendid company."[8] With a number of the young men getting married, Sam confided to his mother that he must soon look for a wife himself, asking what she thought of the idea.

Sam's first Christmas at Heart's Content was one to remember:

> I enjoyed my Christmas very much – we had a gay time here. Quite an extensive dinner at our house after which all the Ladies and Gentlemen of the staff assembled at the office where we enjoyed the night splendidly dancing and singing etc. etc. We had a piano moved to the office for the occasion, Mrs. Woodcock an English lady being a splendid performer. I accommodated the crowd by giving up my room to them as reception room, also for the ladies to arrange their hair, etc. for which it came in very handy, being in the same building as the office. We had a large supper table laid out in it about 11 o'clock & as for wines brandy and champaigne etc. there was no scarcity. Wish you could have heard some of the songs that were sung. Mr. Trippe one of the English staff is a beautiful singer and gave us a few charming songs. It was something different from my last Christmas among the Gaultois youngsters & Indians at Conne River. This is a great place for mummers – crowds of them out all Christmas times. I think it a beastly practice & should be done away with.[9]

The next summer brought additional Anglo staff, including Isaac Angel, who added more musical talent to the mix. Relaxing on a Sunday in August, Sam wrote, "I have been listening to him all the evening playing sacred music & a lot of young men singing."[10] Angel was at once put to work playing in the church where he remained as organist for many years. The summer of 1869 also brought a great many sightseers to Heart's Content, principally "Yankees and

Foreigners," but also some of the upper crust of St. John's – merchants, officers, editors and government officials. According to Sam, "This is getting quite a nobby place."[11] With accommodations in short supply they were all hosted by the staff, hospitality that was returned when any of them visited St. John's. "A man from Heart's Content is quite a lion in St. John's now," declared Sam.[12]

That fall saw a general election in Newfoundland, fought on the question of joining the new confederation of Canada. "Confederation & nonconfederation is in the mouths of all from the merchant to the pauper, and as far as I can judge in this quarter confederation will come out at the small end of the horn," Sam told his father.[13] Indeed it did. There was support in some quarters, but anti-confederate Charles Fox Bennet, a keen propagandist, stoked the fire of independence and successfully thwarted any possibility of union. The confederation proposition was roundly defeated by the election of Bennet's party on November 13. "The excitement of elections is over," Sam reported, "and the Antis have gained the day by a large majority which I am very sorry for."[14]

Every July 27 was a gala day in Heart's Content, marking the anniversary of the cable landing.

> The cable picnic here on the 27th was a grand affair. We gave a treat to all the Sunday School children – such as tea, cake, nuts, apples etc. also a boat race to the natives. It was a general holiday here, the fishermen's society walked etc. We had a lot of guests from St. John's and Harbour Grace, got up a play for their amusement, also a concert & gave them a ball in our office after all the business was thro' (it being the only room in the place large enough). The play was entitled "The Queer Subject," and a laughable thing it was. I took a part in it and did it handsomely. The whole affair went off well & we got great praise from the audience...[15]

Put in perspective, all of this was happening at a time when the fishery was still struggling through one of the worst periods in its history. We can only imagine what the quiet and diffident fishermen made of all the goings on. It is apparent, though, that the staff did what they could to help alleviate the plight of the less fortunate.

Sam observed that the winter of 1868-69 had been fearfully hard on the community, with codfish worth almost nothing in St. John's. Construction of the cable apartments and a company pier that summer would provide work for a great many. Still, a lot of people were "in a miserable state of poverty."[16] The next winter was not much better. Three weeks after the sumptuous Christmas celebration enjoyed by the staff, Ezra Weedon wrote to general manager Richard Collett in London: "...owing to increase in price of provisions and bad times generally we have a number of people about us in a state of semi-starvation. We are doing all we can but that is not much divided among so many. Perhaps if you were to ask Mr. Deane he might do a little privately for them."[17] Collett replied that the Board of Anglo-American was unable to do anything for the poor of Heart's Content, seeing as the shareholders of the company were not yet getting their full dividend.

The times improved in 1870, with a good seal hunt and shore fishery and some success on the coast of Labrador. The market for fish rallied and the economy began to come around. Shopkeepers were selling goods that had lingered on their shelves for 10 years or more. But that fall the failure of Ridley & Company at Harbour Grace was a blow to hundreds of people:

> It happened at a bad time of year, most of his dealers had given in their summer voyage and hadn't taken their winter supply – this harbour has suffered severely. It was supposed they would compromise with their creditors and carry on again but it seems they are quite insolvent. Lots of people in Hbr Grace that had a little money in the bank were offered 6% by Ridleys House within the last 2 years, drew it & gave it to Ridley for the sake of the extra percentage & of course lost all. A place like Oderin t'would be a godsend for a merchant to fail as most of the people would be in debt, but where people are independent & generally have money on the merchant's books it is quite a calamity.[18]

The Ridley bankruptcy closed their branch store at Heart's Content, wiping out credits owing to the planters and fishermen and removing a major source of supply to the trade. Eventually Jillard Brothers of Harbour Grace opened to fill the gap.

At the cable station, life went on. The men played billiards, relaxed in the library, got up some theatre, bought another round of drinks. Several of them, including Sam, joined the newly chartered Masonic Lodge in Harbour Grace. At one point they were taking French lessons: "We have a French teacher here – some 8 or 10 of us go to him 3 times a week 2 hours each class."[19] For their amusement, they put together a few issues of a tongue-in-cheek broadsheet, the *Heart's Content Aurora and New Perlican Trumpet*, reviewed in kind by a like-minded St. John's editor:

> A friend at Heart's Content has kindly forwarded to us a copy of a new paper recently issued there, entitled *The Heart's Content Aurora and New Perlican Trumpet*, and having for motto "Omnia cum grano salis capienda" [Everything to be taken with a grain of salt]. It is a tastefully arranged and well printed eight column folio sheet, on stout demy paper, the contents being all original.
>
> The *Roarer and Blower* (we condense the title for convenience sake, not by any means as a token of disrespect, but because we should like to get to bed before daylight) is not intended as a newspaper, but rather as a safety-valve whereby may escape the exuberant comics of the jolly dogs of Cable Terrace, who otherwise would run very great danger of bursting their respective boilers. The *R. and B.* (that's shorter) is, the public will regret to learn, printed for private circulation only – these Cable Terracemen thus proving themselves to be to some extent aristocrats and exclusives.[20]

In 1870 the *New York Times* looked in again - this time the new apartments and recreational pursuits of the operators more than measured up:

> Beside that beautiful inlet of the sea, wherein the *Great Eastern* sailed in triumph on a memorable day in July, 1866, to herald one of the grandest successes which science has achieved in our days, is raised the new *depôt* of the telegraph operators of Heart's Content. This building is made of freestone and Hamburg brick, and executed with the highest artistic

skill procurable in the island and imported from the other provinces ... Each operator has a *suite* of rooms, neatly furnished and provided with all the necessities of a gentleman's apartments. Servants being hired at extremely low wages in Newfoundland, and the operators being paid at the standard European and American rates, they are well provided with attendants, and are never compelled to "rough it in the bush"...

During midsummer the operators celebrate their annual *fête*, to which the elite of St. John's and Harbour Grace, the only towns of any importance in Newfoundland, are always invited. At this *fête* or picnic the *depôt* is thronged with the flags of every nation and national mottoes during the day, and at night illuminated with Chinese lanterns of every shade, and enlivened by music and a continual display of fireworks ... Cricket, foot races, boat races on the beautiful bay, the slippery pole, and quoit pitching are the principal outdoor amusements at Heart's Content on a *fête* day.[21]

The clipping was forwarded to Ezra Weedon by Henry Weaver, now Anglo's general manager in London, with the comment, "After this article has been well [circulated] in England, I shall have no trouble in obtaining candidates for Heart's Content, which seems to be a most happy name for so enviable a locality."[22]

On June 27, 1873, there was further cause for celebration when the *Great Eastern* steamed into Heart's Content, landing a new cable to replace the 1865 that had weakened and run its course. Again crowds poured in to see the great ship. Sam Bailey told his mother:

You couldn't get a room for love or money. I gave mine to a party of Ladies and laid on the floor for some time. The Great Eastern coming into the Harbour was a very fine sight. We could see her masts over the low land of Northern Point before she appeared herself and as she was decked with flags she presented a magnificent appearance. I was disappointed in her size – thought she would look a great deal larger. But after going on board you could see how big she was, esp. the grand saloon.[23]

The *Great Eastern* stayed through the month of July. With the place packed with visitors there were some uneasy moments when a large fire raging in the woods behind Heart's Content threatened the town. On July 12, the Mizzen Hill was all ablaze, and the fire moved closer the next day. Fortunately, a change in the wind and three days of rain removed the danger, and the festivities resumed.[24]

Alexander M. Mackay (1834-1905). *Courtesy PANL.*

Cyrus Field was back, reconnecting with the *Great Eastern* and paving the way with the Newfoundland government for the impending purchase of the New York, Newfoundland and London Telegraph Company by Anglo-American. The merger of the two companies would bring the Newfoundland telegraph lines and the Cape Breton cable under Anglo control, consolidating their position in Newfoundland. The monopoly on telegraphic communication granted to Field's company in 1854 also passed to Anglo-American. The proposed merger of operations raised questions about who would run the Heart's Content station, and indeed about future management of the telegraph in the colony. It presented an opportunity for some jostling by Ezra Weedon to head up Anglo's combined operations in Newfoundland.

The year before, when word of a possible takeover first came, Weedon had taken the initiative to provide head office with a detailed analysis of the troublesome landline across Newfoundland and the cable connection to Sydney, recommending that the American company would be better off replacing the service with a submarine cable from Placentia to Cape Breton. Alexander Mackay advised otherwise. Weedon fumed that Mackay did not want to see the landline abandoned because of ties with the company supplying provisions to the stations along the line. He was also part owner of the *Merlin*, the vessel used for repair work on the Cabot Strait cable. Apparently, Mackay was not above seeking personal profit from the company's business, and Weedon did not hide his distaste for the practice.

With the amalgamation complete, however, Mackay, shrewd and well connected, emerged as superintendent of Anglo-American in Newfoundland, a position he would hold for the rest of his life. Weedon had to be content with running the Heart's Content station.

Here the merger of the two offices did not go smoothly. According to Weedon, Mackay was "evasive and double-dealing,"[25] throwing every obstacle he could in his path. "It requires me to have all my wits about me to counteract any scheming and plotting that may be going on," Weedon wrote.[26]

Anglo's general manager Henry Weaver was well aware of the intrigue and advised Weedon to be careful how he treated Mackay. "We have got a very difficult game to play in Newfoundland. Mr. Mackay is necessary to us, and we must try and keep him in good humour."[27] The company clearly valued Mackay's position of influence in St. John's and ordered Weedon to settle down and get along with him: "Don't get suspicious of everybody, avoid this, as it will only worry you. Keep your eyes open, and be discreet."[28]

Sam Bailey was delighted with the changeover: "...instead of being under Yankee rule now I am under English. I like it better as there is something sterling about the Britishers."[29] Before 1873 was over, Anglo replaced the trans-island telegraph with a new cable connecting Placentia and Sydney, as Weedon had recommended, and there was talk of a new office building for Heart's Content. The station had grown to 29 employees, 16 of them family men. Some of the foreigners, who had joined in the adventure of the cable landing with no thought of staying permanently, were bringing brides over from England and starting to put down roots. Like Ezra Weedon, who realized that he was likely to be here for a while, they began to turn their attention to bettering their lot in Heart's Content.

Chapter 6

Company Town

Ezra Weedon presided over the integrated operations of Anglo-American from 1873 until his death in 1884. He remained a dedicated company man who looked after his staff and was well regarded in return. They referred to him fondly as "the governor," a title carried by superintendents who came after him. "Your staff on leave were a nice happy lot of fellows," wrote Anglo secretary John Grant from London in 1871, "and if you deserve, as I am sure you do, all the kind things they say of you, you are indeed the happy father of a very happy and contented family..."[1] Weedon's popularity with the staff concerned General Manager Henry Weaver, however, who cautioned: "The great fault you have...in all matters connected with the staff is 'sticking up for your men' – this may be an admirable quality, but when you become a manager, it should be kept in subservience to the interests of the company."[2]

Weedon's time as superintendent was a period of rapid expansion for both the cable station and the community. Though beset by a degenerative illness and dogged by personal tragedy, he threw himself into his work. He oversaw the completion of a new office building and elegant new housing for the staff plus the installation of a modern water system through the town. At the same time, he took charge of building a new school and began the campaign for a grand new church for St. Mary's. In the process he completed the makeover of Heart's Content from a quiet fishing village to a cosmopolitan little place of international stature.

His health problems began as the days were warming in the early summer of 1871. Out on a carriage ride he had a sudden upset when a shaft broke and the horse ran free, pitching him over the dashboard. The accident left him shaken for the rest of the summer. In August, he left with George Charlton for a two-month holiday in Canada and the United States. "If my health has improved," he told head office, "I shall get married on my return, which step will I think be beneficial to me in every way."[3]

He came back refreshed, and in October married 19-year-old Margaret Rutherford of the Rutherford merchant family of Harbour Grace. Sam Bailey, who would later wed Margaret's sister Elizabeth, described how the community welcomed the newlyweds on their late-afternoon arrival at Heart's Content:

> They were met at the entrance of the harbour by nearly all the people here, who took the horse from the carriage and drew them (the bride & bridegroom) through the village amid the biggest caranonading [sic], ringing of bells, dogs barking & hurrahing I've ever seen. Mr. Weedon has been very charitable to the poor here & they did their best to show how they appreciated him. He gave them 10 gallons of rum the next night to drink his health & the whole village got on the bust – 'twas the greatest spree I've seen since I've been here.[4]

It was indeed an auspicious beginning for the new couple, but misfortune was not far behind. By 1874, Weedon's health was again impaired and he was complaining of severe pain in his feet and legs. His young wife was also unwell, battling tuberculosis, a dreaded plague of the nineteenth century. She died in April 1875, leaving two small daughters in his care. Three years later came a second marriage to Sarah Helena (Lily), daughter of Reverend Edward Colley of Topsail. Weedon's pain was by this time unrelenting, and he became incapacitated, getting about on crutches for a while and then in a special invalid carriage. In 1879 he lost one of his daughters. Lily gave him three more girls and a boy, who died in 1884 just a few months before his father. But despite the setbacks, with the steady hand of second-in-command Frank Perry behind him, he was able to stay the course as station superintendent to the very end.

Weedon's first priority after the merger of the two companies in 1873 was to provide better working conditions for the staff. The temporary wood-frame office erected in the fall of 1866, put up in a hurry, was draughty, shaky and almost impossible to keep warm in the winter. The company kept a man on night watch to tend the fires in frosty weather, but even then the wind sliced through the cracks and the batteries sometimes froze solid. Snow blew into the attic and melted through the ceiling. The flimsy one-inch partition dividing the cable and land offices rattled and shook whenever the door opened in a gale of wind. The men kept it in place by jamming desks up against it on both sides.

In 1874, at Weedon's urging, the company purchased additional land from the Hopkins family and commissioned plans for a new building. The contract again went to the Southcotts of St. John's who started work in the summer of 1875. Progress was slow. Even after the building of Cable Terrace, the local men were not attuned to the routine of a construction site. Free-spirited fishermen who were quick and sure-footed on the water were apparently anything but swift when working under a labour foreman from St. John's. Weedon had already pegged them as being too slow at everything, and their female counterparts serving as domestic servants as a lazy lot. On this project, the men turned unruly. Delays from sickness, drunkenness and strikes plagued construction of the new building. By the time the roof was on in December, bad weather halted work for the year.

It was another brutally cold winter. There were days in February when, even with the largest fires going in all the grates, the apartments at Cable Terrace did not get above 28F. A disgruntled and pain-stricken Ezra Weedon told the company that the health of his entire staff was precarious and complained that, of all their stations, Heart's Content had to be the most difficult place to work. They had to put up with seven months of winter, January and February being almost unbearable, and with everyone shut indoors a monotony was created "as great as if on board ship for months together without entering port."[5]

Even so, they were spared the plight facing many local families, still suffering the effects of a meagre fishery and forced to trudge back and forth to the nearest relieving officer in Carbonear for poor rations. The schoolmaster described their ordeal:

> ...last year's long and dreary winter was followed by a late, cold spring. The drift ice hovering about the coast filled our harbours and bays, stopping all navigation, cutting off communications by water with St. John's till nearly the end of May. This was a real trial to our people, and it was heartrending to see the groups of poor footsore men and boys tramping through our streets from the adjacent settlements to and from Carbonear, a distance of about 20 or 30 miles (there and back), bringing in bags on their backs enough flour to last themselves and their families only a few days, then to repeat the same dreary labor and journey...[6]

The cable station opened in 1876, with extensions added 1881. This photo 1898. *Courtesy Claude Rockwood.*

The people of Heart's Content, though by no means well off, stayed above the line of absolute destitution. Government subsidies had sparked a revival of sorts in shipbuilding. This, along with piecework provided by several businesses and the station, plus the charity of the cable staff, helped pull the community through the lean months.

The dismal winter of 1876 finally ended, spirits revived, and work resumed on the new office building. It was finally ready by fall - a handsome 1½-storey red brick structure with stone facings, gingerbread trim and a steep slate roof. The masonry building made a statement, giving Anglo-American a commanding presence in the centre of town and reinforcing its dominant position in the community. For the staff, the work environment was much improved – no shaking of partitions here – with an up-to-date plaster-finished interior, hardwood floors and varnished wainscot. Separate work areas accommodated the cable and land operations. The mirror galvanometers in the cable section were mounted on individual iron or brick pedestals resting on solid ground and protruding up through the floor. There was also a new invention by William Thomson, the siphon galvanometer or "recorder." This latest device created a permanent record of the cable signals with left/right deflections of an automatic pen on a moving paper tape, increasing the reception speed from eight to ten words per minute and eliminating the need for a second operator. It served as the standard receiving instrument on ocean cables for over 40 years.

In the land office, the telegraph keys and sounders sat on a large table, their clatter filling the room 24 hours a day. The station was a tourist draw and its "glittering medley of brasswork, keys and keyboards, wheels, jars, wires, and general telegraphic paraphernalia"[7] made an impression on all who came to visit. The gentlemen of the staff were genial hosts, unfailingly courteous, and grateful, one supposes, to those who showed up to help break the tedium of the everyday grind.

With the move to the new office, the old building was turned over to the staff who converted it to a recreation and entertainment center renamed the Variety Hall. The Fishermen's Hall and later the Orange Hall, opened in 1881 by the Loyal Orange Association, provided venues for the suppers, concerts and dances that made up the social life of the community. The Variety Hall served the same function for the station employees.

Heart's Content in 1876 was the terminus of three operating cables: the 1866, the 1873 and a third laid west-to-east by the *Great Eastern* on her final cable voyage in 1874. The inferior 1865 cable was by now discontinued. There was also a cable trenched across the isthmus of the Avalon Peninsula to Placentia Bay, where it connected to the submarine cable to Sydney laid in 1873. The 1866 cable was replaced by a new line to Valentia in 1880. Meanwhile, competition on the transatlantic route was increasing. In 1874 the Direct United States Telegraph Co. brought a cable to the entrance of Trinity Bay, but were forced to divert to Nova Scotia when Anglo enforced its monopoly on cable landings. Five years later the *Compaignie Francaise du Telegraphe de Paris à New-York* laid a cable from Brest to St. Pierre with connections to Cape Breton and Cape Cod.[8]

At this point, Heart's Content was well able to compete, with improvements at the station keeping it at the forefront of the industry. After Thomson's recorder, the next enhancement was duplexing, a development that greatly improved the capacity of the cables by allowing messages to pass simultaneously in both directions. The duplex system adopted by Anglo-American required installation of an "artificial line," an arrangement of resistors and capacitors set up to mimic the electrical characteristics of the cable. When the artificial line was balanced electrically with the cable, creating a Wheatstone bridge, operators could receive incoming messages with no interference from messages going out. A rear extension was added to the office building in 1881 to house the new duplexing equipment.

Thomson's recorder, introduced in 1874, traced a permanent record of cable messages on a paper tape. *From Field (1893).*

The staff were also quick to latch on to other advances in communication, the telephone being a prime example. Alexander Graham Bell perfected his "talking telegraph" in 1876, details of which appeared in the March 1877 issue of *Scientific American.* In a world where the telephone was still very much a rarity, the staff acquired or built their own sets and connected up with Placentia over the telegraph line. The first telephone call in Newfoundland went through from Heart's Content to Placentia on January 20, 1878. The *Harbour Grace Standard* reported: "the instrument worked admirably, the operator speaking at one end making himself clearly understood at the other."[9]   Later that year, Anglo superintendent Alexander Mackay installed the first private telephone line in St. John's, and in 1885 set up the first telephone exchange in the city on behalf of the company.

By 1880 the expanded workforce at the Heart's Content station was putting a squeeze on housing. By now there were 24 married men on staff – nine living in company housing, three with houses of their own, and 12 in rental accommodation. Weedon addressed the housing problem with plans and specifications for six new two-storey houses, three on the main road and three more at the top of the hill behind the office with a sweeping view of the upper harbour. The contract went to architect John T. Southcott, second generation of the St. John's building firm. The homes were designed in the fashionable Second-Empire style favoured by the well-to-do of St. John's and added a decided flair to the look and feel of the community. Weedon, who was living in Cable Terrace, had the superintendent's house designed a little larger than the others, with two extra rooms on the main floor so that he would not have to use the stairs.

The summer of 1881 was wet - not good for construction or Weedon's health - and he was unable to get around to keep a close eye on the project. Again work proceeded at a snail's pace. The houses were closed in just before the end of the year, and the inside work proceeded through the winter. Five were ready by the end of 1882; it took another seven months to finish Weedon's. As with Cable Terrace, the houses were equipped with fine furniture and appointments imported from England. Sam Bailey moved into the house next to the superintendent, naming it "Sunny Brae." Weedon called his "Mount Pleasant."

While plans for the new houses were underway, Heart's Content fell under the dark cloud of diphtheria, forcing a modernization of water services. In November 1880, Dr. William Anderson, Anglo's medical officer, answered a call to Southern Cove to find a boy rapidly expiring from diphtheria. Anderson was able to save the youngster by emergency procedure: inserting a tube in his windpipe and sucking out the

Weedon's house and two others built 1882-83. This photo c.1919. *Courtesy Western Union Telegraph Company Records, Archives Center, National Museum of American History, Smithsonian Institution.*

obstructing blood and mucus. Shortly after, another child in a nearby house was infected, with death coming so swiftly that there was no time to get the doctor in. The affected families were placed under quarantine and the usual precautions taken (boiling drinking water, daily fumigation of dwelling-houses and removal of all foul matter from their vicinity), but within weeks Heart's Content found itself in the middle of a full-blown epidemic.

Dr. William Anderson (1846-1897). *Courtesy Dr. Nigel Rusted.*

As the disease spread, people tried their own home remedies. They rubbed kerosene oil on the throat of a sick child or gave it orally as a medicine. Placing a hot roasted herring (a "Labrador turkey") on the throat was another treatment.[10]   Dr. Anderson, a large, robust man and expert physician, juggled as many as 11 cases at a time. In all, some 85 people in 30 families were stricken, most of them children. The quiet procession trudging to the graveyard behind a tiny coffin became an all-too-familiar sight – on one day alone there were three separate burials. By mid-January, 30 children had died, including three from families of the cable station.

Diphtheria spread rapidly where the drinking water was contaminated. At Cable Terrace, problems with the water supply went back to 1871, when the common well servicing the apartments was found to be unfit. Individual wells were dug in the basement of each house and this worked for a while, but within a few years they were also condemned, and the servants were going off to fetch drinking water from the Main Brook.

When the diphtheria epidemic ended in 1881, Weedon lobbied the company to clean up the water supply once and for all. They eventually agreed to a gravity-fed system from Southern Cove Pond. *The Heart's Content Water Supply Act*, passed by the Newfoundland legislature in April 1883, gave Anglo-American the right to install and maintain a waterline through the community and the right to protect the water supply. Ownership and administration of the water system remained with the company.

Running water was a luxury enjoyed by few people in North America, let alone Newfoundland where only St. John's and Harbour Grace had a public water supply. Almost a century would pass before most outports, including those close to Heart's Content, had water piped in. All the more remarkable that the summer of 1883 found Anglo-American installing a system through Heart's Content. The project proceeded under the supervision of S. T. Morgan, an engineer brought in from England, at a cost of £3,000. At the height of construction in August, 100 men and three boys were bustling about digging trenches and laying pipe. Weedon was wheeled over to Southern Cove in his invalid carriage to inspect their progress. The waterline reached the cable office on November 1, where Dickenson, the inventive station mechanician, had a small turbine assembled to power his lathes. The service was connected to all houses occupied by the staff, and Southcott was called back to install plumbing in those finished the year before.

When Morgan left for England at the end of the year the system was not quite complete, and he made plans to return in the spring to finish the job. Over the summer a romance had blossomed with Miss Woodworth, the schoolmistress, with an engagement announced before he left. Morgan had also developed an interest in mineral exploration in Newfoundland. Weedon saw no need to bring him back. "No doubt he wants to come back at company's expense…" he wrote head office. "I think he wants a snug berth here as 'water engineer' at a good salary which would leave him plenty of time for mine-hunting."[11] Apparently that was the last they saw of him, and the last anyone heard of Miss Woodworth's wedding plans. Charlton finished the waterline and looked after it for the company.

Anglo-American's water system ran a distance of some 8,000 feet from Southern Cove Pond to the Fishermen's Hall, with branches to the company houses on the higher levels. Fire hydrants were installed on the line, and the company kept a mobile fire hose stored in a small shed across from Cable Terrace. Later on they added a community alarm system, with a horn over the front entrance of the office building connected to remote alarm boxes. Before construction started on the waterline the company had approached the government to share the cost of installation for homes outside the cable circle, but their proposal was turned down. Anglo then offered townspeople the right to buy a lifetime hook-up for £10, but that was beyond the reach of most of them, and no one did. A few homes in the centre of town owned by the merchant families of Hopkins and Moore were allowed to tie in at cost (about £5), as the line was laid past their doors. Other than that, the only houses serviced were those occupied by the staff.

While the line was going in the company again contacted government to have the service extended to the planters and fishermen of Rowe's Bank, where crowded housing was also polluting the wells, and on to Northern Point. The only commitment they could get was £60 to install four running hydrants along the line for public use, one with a drinking trough for the horses. Not satisfied with that, the homeowners beyond the Fishermen's Hall petitioned for an extension to the line. At the last minute, in November, funding came through to take the line a further 900 feet, with two more running hydrants. The system ended at the home of John Farnham, the Anglo battery man, at the far end of Rowe's Bank.

Through the years, company control of the water supply rankled the rest of the community. The locals could not work at the office or live in the company houses, but they could certainly benefit from running water had they been allowed. Like other outport communities, the people of Heart's Content had always freely shared the resources of land and sea. The company's refusal to grant the right to a basic commodity like fresh water ran counter to the prevailing ethic. Once the system went in, however, Anglo stood firm in controlling access. A few hook-ups were made from time to time under the cover of darkness, and the company, perhaps wisely, turned a blind eye. But restrictions on the water supply remained a sore point right up to the time the station closed.

Completion of a new office building and six eye-catching houses, plus the water supply, firmly fixed Anglo-American's stamp on Heart's Content, moving it well beyond the typical outport where the fishery pervaded all. However, company projects were only part of the picture. Anglo's presence spilled over into wider aspects of community life, and dominated those as well.

Chapter 7

Higher Standards

The Heart's Content winters that were such a discomfort for the Englishmen nonetheless worked wonders for the birth rate. Many who had joined in the adventure of the cable laying with little thought of taking up permanent residence in Newfoundland were bringing brides over from England and putting down roots. By December 1875, there were 45 children among the cable families, and they were arriving at a rate of about one a month. Already 10 were of school age. Ezra Weedon, widowed with two small daughters of his own, had schooling very much on his mind. He considered what Heart's Content had to offer.

The schoolhouse built in 1862 still operated under the auspices of the CCCS – the Colonial and Continental Church Society – with 80-90 students enrolled. Typical of nineteenth-century schooling, attendance over the years had been spotty and the level of instruction mediocre at best. J. W. Marriott, appointed school inspector for the colony in 1859, offered this assessment of Newfoundland schools:

> Without exception I found the subjects which the masters professed to take up rather limited…[instruction] goes no further than simple reading and writing, with the religious teaching from the Bible and Church Catechism, and a very small amount of arithmetic. No grammar, no secular history, no geography, no object lessons, nor any music except the singing of simple hymns from ear, in a few instances, and, in one case, of a few school songs.[1]

Captain John Orlebar, a patron of the CCCS, made an inspection of the Heart's Content school during the cable survey of 1864. He was unimpressed with the efforts of schoolmaster William Thompson who was being paid an extra stipend to teach navigation. Marriott considered Thompson very industrious and found the children getting on well in reading and arithmetic, but he was relieved of his duties all the same. His replacement, a young schoolmistress from St. John's, described the students, especially the younger ones, as being in "a very backward state. Owing to removal in prosecuting the Labrador fishery, many of them are taken away just at the time when they ought most to attend to their studies."[2]   As far as the fishermen were concerned, it was fine for their children to go to school as long as it did not interfere with the fishing.

In 1869, James Gardner, father of the clergyman George Gardner and long-time veteran of the CCCS, took charge of the school at Heart's Content.   Formerly a plumber and glazier of Bedfordshire, James Gardner was teaching school in London when he and his wife offered themselves as missionary teachers in 1851 and shipped out with their family to Harbour Grace.   In Newfoundland they garnered a reputation as exemplary teachers, even spending a few years at the Society's Central School in St. John's that served as a teacher-training institute.   Now recently widowed, and wishing that "his employment be more of a missionary character,"[3] James Gardner joined his son at Heart's Content, bringing along the rest of his family, James Jr., Emma and Mary.   They took up residence in the old Underhay plantation house across the road from St. Mary's.   Gardner began lay reading in the church and Emma became his assistant at the school. Within a few years, both daughters married into the cable circle.

The CCCS paid Gardner's salary, but the school had to get by on whatever meagre resources the townspeople could provide.   Most of them could pay little in the way of tuition, which was optional, but every day the children brought wood for the stove.   In 1870 the men got together, clapboarded and painted the schoolhouse and tarred the roof, all with free labour. Tuition collected for the year amounted to a scant £12.   The vicious winter of 1875 brought less than that, as Gardner reported to the Society:

> I am sorry to say that many more children might be gathered both in the day and Sunday school, but in many instances the poor children have not clothes to come in, the fisheries have of late been so poor that their parents have not the means to supply their wants. This also accounts for the small amount of fees collected. I am compelled to take in numbers free, otherwise they would receive no education at all.[4]

This was not a school for the children of the cable staff. Ezra Weedon called the parents together in the library on December 27, 1875, to discuss the question of schooling. The next day he wrote the company outlining their predicament with Gardner and the CCCS School:

> There is a school here but of the poorest kind; it is much lower in the scale than the lowest National School at home, and in every way unsuited for our requirements. In addition to the Schoolmaster being imperfectly educated, the moral tone of the school is very low indeed; therefore the opinion is unanimous that no education at all is preferable to sending the children to such a school as this.[5]

National Schools were elementary schools in rural villages of England, operated by the National Society for Promoting the Education of the Poor, at the bottom of the education system. In Heart's Content the only alternative left for the cable staff was to start a school of their own, but the parents could reach no agreement as to how it should be financed. Weedon took the matter in hand and with four others (Dickenson, Bailey, Charlton and James) formed the Heart's Content School Association. They issued 50 shares at £10 each, attracting 23 shareholders, all from Anglo families. The company agreed to an annual grant of £20, and the schoolhouse, a tidy little one-room affair, was ready by the end of 1876. The notion of a private school, built by private subscription and charging an annual tuition of £5, was a contentious issue. At the opening on December 26, 1876, Ezra Weedon – all 4½ feet of him – was as feisty as ever:

> Some twelve months ago, at a meeting held in the Anglo-American Telegraph Company's Library, I guaranteed that a School should be built: here it is...We have had a great deal of up-hill work to do, and much opposition to contend with, before reaching our present position. We have been abused on all sides; accused of all manner of mean actions and uncharitable motives. Fortunately, we can bear a lot of that kind of thing; in fact, we are getting so accustomed to it that it comes natural to us...Some people express an opinion that we are going to make a lot of money out of the School. I hope we may; but I fail to see how it's to be made, or where it's to come from...It appears to me

that for the next four or five years all the financial meetings convened by the Secretary will be for the purpose
of making calls to cover deficits; this we expected from
the first, and we are prepared to lose money for a few
years, provided that we gain our object and organize a
good School. Now I hope none of you will misunder-
stand my last remarks and think that I am begging or
soliciting you to send your children to school, because
I am doing no such thing; begging is not our policy…[6]

The school was a business investment and Weedon made it clear
that, as long as the tuition could be met, they would welcome children
from any family. It was a hollow invitation for most of the townspeople, though, who the year before had barely managed £5 altogether in
tuition fees for the CCCS. Still, four of the 18 pupils who started in
January were the children of more prosperous planters who had no
connection with the station.

The teacher they hired was Abbie L. Fleming, a young Nova Scotian
who had introduced the progressive curriculum of that province to
Newfoundland six years earlier at the private Victoria Street School in
Harbour Grace. Her work was widely admired and her school
acclaimed as one of the leading educational institutions on the island.
She was certainly a "catch" for the school at Heart's Content. There
her reputation remained stellar as she raised the educational standard
(and presumably the moral tone) to meet the expectations of the staff.

In September 1879, Abbie Fleming made Heart's Content home by
marrying 47-year-old George Charlton of the cable station in a ceremony at Harbour Grace. It was nothing to match the reception accorded
Weedon eight years before, but the bride and groom arrived home to
find their house festooned with flags and arches and the children waiting with their wedding gift.[7] The school now had 16 students, three
from outside the office. Unfortunately, the custom of the times did not
sanction careers for married ladies, and they were left without a teacher.

By this time, however, James Gardner had stepped down at the
CCCS School and handed the reins to his assistant George Adams, a
clever young scholar receiving accolades from the school inspector for
managing "the best Church of England common school in the
Island."[8] Apparently he was also good enough for some of the staff,
who could now enjoy the best of both worlds: a first-rate teacher at little or no cost.

Lakeview School 1896.

In 1881, more than 20 children of Anglo families were attending class under Adams, and the shareholders of the private school were sitting with no teacher and an empty building on their hands. When Ezra Weedon, his health in decline, resigned as president of the School Association, the shareholders moved to regroup. A few days after Weedon's resignation in April 1882, they elected a management committee, headed by Charles Trippe, to put the school back in operation.[9] The committee wanted to hire a schoolmaster from England, but this was an expense the shareholders were unwilling to assume. Instead, they brought in another young mistress from Nova Scotia, a Miss Woodworth, at a salary of $400. The school reopened on May 1. Anglo children trotted back from the CCCS School and new pupils came in, bringing the enrolment to 38.

The committee took charge of running the school, which they named Lakeview. They drew up a set of operating procedures, dividing the children into first, second and third classes according to their age and the subjects taken, and established a new scale of fees. The holiday schedule was set at four weeks in the summer, a fortnight at Christmas, plus Good Friday and Easter Monday. There was a public examination at Christmas. The committee visited the school every three months, and they asked William Pilot, the inspector of Church of England schools, to carry out an annual inspection.

They also provided an assistant for the teacher, and the next three years went well, the shareholders receiving a small dividend on their investment. Then Miss Woodworth asked for a salary increase in return for extra teaching. The committee waffled, at first refusing but then agreeing on condition that they terminate her assistant. Frustrated, and perhaps still stinging from the affair with the waterworks engineer, Miss Woodworth was in no mood to bargain. She resigned, packed her bags and left.

There followed a period of turmoil and unrest at the school, firmly demonstrating the folly of management by committee. Four new teachers came and went in four years. What the shareholders wanted was an English schoolmaster. They considered it beyond their means to get one, but they seemed unable to satisfy themselves with anything less. Without Weedon's leadership, they were floundering. They meddled in matters that were better left to the teacher and bickered among themselves. If a family took a dislike to the teacher, they took their children out of school and refused to pay their fees.

In this environment the management committee had its hands full, trying to shoulder disciplinary as well as administrative problems. Many of the students were now in their teens and exhibiting more than a passing interest in the other sex:

> ... to keep the boys and girls separate outside the schoolroom it was agreed to put up a board fence setting apart a portion of the ground for exclusive use of girls and that WCs at back of school should be used by the girls only – a new one to be erected for the boys. It was agreed that any boys found in the girls' playground or WCs should be severely punished for the first offence & expelled for the second.[10]

A meeting of the committee in February 1889 recorded the following:

> A difficulty having arisen between Mr. Bellamy & Miss Elmsley concerning the way in which Florence Bellamy was punished on the 21st, and as the secretary was unable to arrange matters to the satisfaction of the parties aggrieved members were called together to give their decision in the dispute.

Mr. Bellamy's letter was intemperately worded and for the threats contained in it an apology was demanded by Miss Elmsley before she would allow the child to return to the school.

The correspondence which had passed between the secretary & parties having been read & considered, Dr. Anderson proposed & Mr. Ed Earle seconded that Miss Elmsley be reprimanded for indiscretion in keeping Florence Bellamy as long out of the schoolroom in the cold air; to express regret for the intemperate tone of Mr. Bellamy's letter; and that the proposal of Mr. Bellamy to allow Florence to finish the quarter under Miss Moore in the Primary Dept. be agreed to. Carried unanimously.[11]

While the parents squabbled at Lakeview, the school of the Colonial and Continental Church Society flourished. In 1886, the Society built a new schoolhouse, "the most commodious and most eligible school we have in the colony for the Church of England,"[12] according to the inspector. To the chagrin of the Lakeview parents, they also appointed an English schoolmaster.

At the end of 1889 the shareholders finally gave up trying to run Lakeview and handed it over to the parents, retaining ownership of the building and grounds. In 1892, the Church of England Board of Education leased the school and took over administration, bringing the private school experiment to an end. The schoolhouse remained the property of the Heart's Content School Association, Anglo-American continued to pay its annual grant, and the shareholders continued to pay dividends to themselves. The Association carried on as a peculiar little enterprise with one real estate asset, its dividends derived from the largesse of the cable company, until the 1950s.

After the bungled attempt at running Lakeview, many cable families took to sending their sons and daughters to boarding school in St. John's, as did some of the merchants. For early schooling, the staff threw in with the rest of the community. They maintained a level of control over the education of their children, however, through representation on the Board of Education and later the School Board. The school was one place where the two classes were forced to coexist. Another was the church.

Chapter 8

Exalted Aspirations

As the cable station expanded and the staff began a permanent settling, their presence reached deeply into the religious life of the one-church community. Traditionally Church of England with perhaps a dozen Irish-Catholic families and a few scattered Methodists, Heart's Content in a short time became home to four new places of worship. The changes were most apparent at St. Mary's, from the church itself to the clergy to the style of worship. At the same time, Methodists at the station organized a congregation, built a church and brought in a minister. The Roman Catholics also came together with a church of their own, and the Salvation Army established a presence through the impassioned work of a cable operator. In the religious life of Heart's Content the impact of the station was all pervasive.

Dickenson's Grand Design

St. Mary's church, completed in 1846, was built by local workmen in the simple, unpretentious style of outport Newfoundland. Enlarged around 1860 and again in 1874, it could accommodate 800 people, more than adequate for the 900 parishioners on the books. The building was beginning to show its age and could do with a little refurbishing, but Weedon and the staff had more ambitious plans. As with the school, the expatriate Englishmen aspired to something better.

St. Mary's Church c.1875.

Once they had the school up and running, they set their sights on a church of their own making.

They were not happy with the church, nor were they pleased with the pastor. George Gardner, social advocate and champion of the needy, practised a "low church" brand of Anglicanism – a simple liturgy with no ceremonial flair and minimal accoutrements. The grand new edifice the Englishmen had in mind was intended to fix that, but Gardner had little interest in attending to the needs of the upper crust of the parish at the expense of the underprivileged. He was spending a lot of time with his congregation at Scilly Cove, where the Wesleyans were making strong inroads. There he founded the Church of England Women's Association as a means, he said, of preventing impressionable young women from straying to the Wesleyan fold. Like the Fishermen's Society of Heart's Content, the C.E.W.A. expanded into an island-wide movement. Gardner spent most of his Sundays combating the Wesleyans at Scilly Cove, leaving his father to attend to services at Heart's Content. Given their assessment of James Gardner as a schoolteacher, this was an arrangement the cable staff would have found less than satisfactory.

In this context, the new church saga began at a meeting of St. Mary's congregation in April 1877. Weedon's minutes show an agenda very much driven by the staff, the locals – or "natives" – displaying their trademark deference to the British:

> The attendance was not satisfactory there being too few of the natives present. The question of putting the graveyard in order was freely discussed and satisfactorily disposed of after which a discussion took place on the Church itself, the question being whether the present Church should be repaired or an attempt made to raise funds to build a new one. The latter met with more support from the Staff than the former, but the natives seemed disinclined to express an opinion either one way or the other. However, on the proposition being put to the meeting that an attempt should be made to raise funds for a new Church the motion was carried without a dissentient voice.[1]

A second meeting in June saw another poor attendance, but produced a decision on a site for the new church on the crown of the hill just behind the existing one. William Dickenson, whose talents extended beyond the bounds of electricity and telegraphy, already had a set of drawings prepared for an elaborate structure of cruciform shape 128 feet in length, 90 feet wide and rising to a height of 77 feet. It would accommodate 1,000 people, cost £2,500 and be the finest wooden church in Newfoundland. Again, the locals were reticent: "the discussion was confined chiefly to the staff and was not so general as could be wished".[2] Still, the meeting approved Dickenson's design and resolved that the church would be built by the people of the harbour under his direction. Fundraising was underway by early December, with money coming in from donors in St. John's, while Weedon solicited contributions from "influential men" in England and America, i.e., the principals of Anglo-American and the former New York, Newfoundland and London Telegraph Company. Many of them, Cyrus Field included, gave generously to the project.

With the staff moving to take charge of church and school affairs, George Gardner was no longer at home in Heart's Content. He left abruptly in July 1878. Having a committee of the congregation involved in church finances may have hastened his going, for in financial affairs he was hopelessly muddled. Weedon later wrote, "Since his departure things have come to light about money matters which reflect anything but credit on him; everything he has the handling of has been found all astray, discrepancies in accounts, amounts overdrawn, etc."[3] It seems Gardner was no more a favourite among the cable clique than his father was as schoolmaster.

If the staff welcomed Gardner's departure, such was not the case with the rest of the community, especially the Fishermen's Society. He was in Colbourne, Ontario in 1881 when they recognized his years of service with a testimonial of £43/12/8, acknowledged in a warm and gracious response:

> Words cannot convey my feelings of thankfulness and gratitude…for such an unexpected expression of regard, accompanied by a handsome sum of money, a tangible proof of the sincerity and good feelings of the donors towards me and while I feel that no services of mine rendered to the Society or any of its members, could in any way, deserve such recognition, for whatever I may have done, was only a duty and a pleasure…I have never forgotten the many happy gatherings with

the brethren I enjoyed in dear old Newfoundland. I
live in hope that, some day, in God's good providence,
I may be permitted to meet with you again...[4]

There is no indication that George Gardner ever returned to
Newfoundland. At Heart's Content he was replaced in 1879 by
Frederick R. Murray from the Cathedral parish in St. John's – British-
educated, high church and well suited to the Englishmen. As soon as
Gardner left, Weedon had the annual clergyman's grant from Anglo-
American raised from £10 to £50.

The new church began to take shape in 1880, with James H. Moore
as master builder under Dickenson's watchful eye. The project provided a summer's work for men of the parish at wages of $1 per day.
The next year, with a busy shore fishery underway, the building committee had to increase the daily wage to keep men on the job putting
on the clapboard. The laying of the cornerstone was set to coincide
with the anniversary of the cable landing: Wednesday, July 27, 1881.

It was another red-letter day for the town and it went off in grand
style. The July weather had been unsettled, but on the morning of the
27th the gods smiled and the sun finally broke through. "Early rising
was the order of the day, and before breakfast fair ladies in pretty
morning dresses might have been seen going about busily preparing
for the reception and comfort of expected visitors, the juvenile members of the community also mustering in great force."[5] Members of
the Masonic Order turned out to support their brethren at the cable
station. Anglo's Alexander Mackay, Provincial Grand Master under
the Scottish Grand Lodge, came to lay the cornerstone. The SS
Leopard arrived just before 9 a.m. after an overnight passage from St.
John's, bringing Mackay and the Masons. From nearby settlements
people streamed in by carriage and on foot.

Five triumphal arches erected throughout the community greeted
the visitors. The Masons went on parade, led by the band of the
British Society from Harbour Grace. They finished up at the new
church, where Mackay lowered the cornerstone in place. The party
then proceeded to the Variety Hall to lunch with the building committee, while others enjoyed refreshments in the Orange Hall across the
road. The sun beamed down on a leisurely afternoon, as the visitors
took time to stroll around town. The cable station was open for tours.
The church women had a Sale of Work in the Fishermen's Hall, where
a special stall featured articles made by the children to raise money for

a new christening font. Just after 6 o'clock the last few stragglers scrambled on board the *Leopard* for the return trip to St. John's. On shore the celebrations continued with a choral concert in the new church organized by organist Isaac Angel, and a variety concert the following evening in the Fishermen's Hall. Supported by a flurry of fancy fairs, concerts and bazaars, work on the church proceeded as funds came in.

C. Ernest Smith (1855-1939).
From Smith (1925).

Reverend Murray left Heart's Content toward the end of 1881, replaced by C. Ernest Smith, another British-trained clergyman and graduate of Oxford. Smith, coming from Harbour Grace, was prepared for what awaited him: a parish of two cultures and two classes, existing side by side. He was not at all prepared, however, for some of the technical wizardry taken for granted at the station. In his memoirs he relates that soon after his arrival Ezra Weedon, now an invalid, asked if he could have a small instrument installed in the church pulpit in order to hear the preacher's sermons at home. Smith had some misgivings but agreed to the arrangement. On Sunday he ascended to the pulpit to find what he would later recognize as a telephone mouthpiece. The telephone was old news at the station, but a very disconcerting novelty to Smith. He found himself unable to concentrate on his sermon, knowing that someone was listening in a few hundred yards away. On Monday, he visited Weedon to find out if he had heard anything, and to his dismay found that everything he said had been relayed perfectly over the phone. The next Sunday was easier, and Smith felt that he would eventually get used to the idea. After a few weeks, however, Weedon decided that the strain of listening in was too great, and had the mouthpiece removed. Smith was relieved.[6] Meanwhile, he adjusted well to another feature of life in the cable town. How many parishes provided a country preacher the luxury of the latest world news delivered to his desk first thing every morning?

The new church was finished during Smith's tenure, though not before a dust-up over the assignment of pews. The system of pew rentals proposed by the building committee favoured the cable staff, and some long-time parishioners who could ill afford to pay stood to be bumped from the more expensive pews at the front of the church.

Smith attempted to settle the issue at a congregational meeting in December 1882. Here a proposal was put forward to leave the question of pews in the hands of the building committee for a final decision. The locals may have been disinclined to express an opinion at church meetings, but they knew how to stymie proceedings if they had to:

> This proposition gave rise to a lengthy discussion during which a great many persons left the meeting. A show of hands being called for by the Rev. Chairman did not give the result – the meeting was apparently about equally divided. Those "for" were asked to stand up & those "against" to remain sitting. This procedure did not seem to be understood & no decision could be arrived at – a count was then proposed with a like result. As a final test those "for" were asked to walk to one side of the building & those "against" to the other. This resulted in greater confusion than before – the Rev. Chairman now declined to press the matter further.[7]

Their distaste for confrontation notwithstanding, the people seemed to have perfected the art of passive resistance. Eventually they got their way when it was decided to leave every alternate pew vacant, allowing those who wished to sit near the front to do so free of charge. It turned out to be a wise decision, since the new church, grand as it was, suffered from poor acoustics. Even with his superior speaking voice and precise British diction Rev. Smith's words were not easily picked up in the back rows.

The pews were in by the spring of 1884, and Smith held the official opening in May before the fishermen left for Labrador. With the bishop away, the consecration had to wait until the end of the season. It was another splendid occasion with Bishop Llewellyn Jones assisted by 10 clergy of the Diocese, followed by more lunching at the Variety Hall. Special praise was accorded William Dickenson for his design and supervision of the project, and Sam Bailey, who had taken over from Weedon on the building committee. "His was not a pleasant post, and few could realize its responsibility and anxiety."[8]

Bringing the church to completion was a huge effort over seven years and the end result did not fail to impress:

St. Mary's Church opened 1884. *Courtesy Blanche and Dorothy Rowe.*

On entering the building the visitor is at once struck
with the lofty and fine proportions. There are six bays
in the nave with pointed gothic arches resting on mas-
sive wooden piers with heavily moulded capitals. The
rose windows of the clerestory are filled with colored
glass. The roof is carried on heavy wooden principals
with tie-beams and purlins, supported on arched ties
resting on handsome wooden corbels. The whole is
stained and varnished throughout. The deep mould-
ings of the arches are finely worked in plaster.[9]

For more than a century, St. Mary's Church was the crowning touch
to the Heart's Content landscape. It vanished in a rush of fire and
smoke on a chilly May evening in 1989:

A 36-year-old Heart's Content man has been charged
with wilfully setting a fire which destroyed the Anglican
Church in that Trinity Bay town last Saturday, May 6...
It took only about two hours for the old building to be
completely razed to the ground. Residents of Heart's
Content, the vast majority of whom are Anglican, were
shocked and saddened at the loss of their historic
church. Because of its prominence on the hill, the
building had also become a familiar landmark to trav-
ellers through the Trinity Bay town.[10]

Methodism Takes Hold

Coinciding with the campaign for a new St. Mary's, Methodism was coming alive in Heart's Content. Prior to 1870, the followers were few: Thomas Hopkins, who had married a Methodist girl from Carbonear, businessman Richard Penney, and Reuben Bemister, a merchant from New Perlican. The three families had quietly nurtured the Wesleyan flame, meeting and holding services in their kitchens.[11]

Methodism took on new life as the cable station expanded. Among the newcomers was Samuel Seymour Stentaford of Brigus, who joined the New York, Newfoundland and London Telegraph Company in 1871. An affable and urbane man, and a top-notch telegrapher, Stentaford quickly gained respect in the cable town. His marriage to Martha Aseneth, daughter of Thomas Hopkins, in 1874 spawned one of the pre-eminent cable families of Heart's Content, producing three generations of workers at the station. Two of their sons went up through the ranks to serve as superintendent, and their grandson was among the last employees when the station closed in 1965.

Stentaford's parents were Congregationalists, but he was a staunch Wesleyan. Under his guidance, with the help of A. A. Thompson of Old Perlican, the Methodist movement advanced to the point where they could bring in their first minister in 1877. Reverend Joseph Lester stayed only a year, but that was long enough to get a church underway. It opened in 1878 with just 22 pews, too few to kindle any dispute over who would sit where. The congregation was especially pleased with the building's excellent acoustical properties, which gave not the slightest unpleasant echo.[12]

Ezra Weedon, in the middle of fundraising for the new St. Mary's, showed more than a little pique at the Methodists' progress. In June 1881, Stentaford, Thompson and Thomas Oates, recently arrived from St. John's, wrote the "governor" requesting a grant from Anglo-American toward a new parsonage. While offering to help them get a subsidy for their minister, Weedon refused support for the parsonage and shot off a blistering tirade that reflected the storm clouds of sectarianism gathering in the community:

> I cannot close this without saying a few words in reference to your Meeting House and the circumstances under which it was built. Neither of you can say with truth that the building was required. Two of you at

Samuel Seymour Stentaford family c.1895. *Courtesy Rick Stentaford.*

Methodist Church c.1921. *Courtesy Hazel Goodridge.*

least know as well as I do that it was built, not because
the number of Wesleyans here was increasing so much
as to render a Meeting House necessary but because it
was anticipated that while we (the Church) were in
trouble through unforeseen and unavoidable circumstances you would be able to induce some of our people to desert the Church. Things did not turn out as
you expected and the consequence is that your
Meeting House is a sort of "White Elephant" a costly
article.

This much for your Meeting House but that is not all.
You who are only a few in number are not only bur-
dened with the cost of keeping up the Meeting House
but since it was built the burden has been increased by
adding to it the cost of your minister's residence. Now
you must excuse me if I say (what every right-minded
man must say) that the residence of your minister
should be where his flock is the thickest, namely Scilly
Cove. He has to go from H.C. to Scilly Cove to preach
there and were he living in Scilly Cove he would have
to travel only the same distance as at present and he
would live where his flock numbers probably 10 to 1 as
compared with H.C. Moreover the large numbers in
Scilly Cove are better able to build a Parsonage than
the few who are here.

There is about as much sense in your minister's headquarters being here as there would be in our
Parsonage being at H. Delight or Scilly Cove.

Of course this is no business of mine but I can't help
speaking my mind on the subject. Things as they stand
at present prove one thing conclusively, namely that
the Wesleyan object in this mission is not exactly to
minister to the Wesleyan wants according to the
Wesleyan numbers but to make all the [inroads possi-
ble] against the "Church". If this were not so your minister's headquarters would be where his flock is thickest, namely Scilly Cove.[13]

No disinclination here in expressing an opinion. There is no doubt
though that the changes underway at St. Mary's were driving parish-

ioners to the Methodist option. Some were half-hearted about the new church project and must have been dismayed at George Gardner's sudden departure. On top of that, they found the high church style and imperious manner of Murray and Smith foreign and intimidating.

Smith's overbearing attitude did not help. He was appalled at the backwardness he perceived in the parish and determined to do something about it:

> In all matters connected with ritual and ceremony they had been and still were in the depths of Puritan bondage. Black stoles, Geneva gowns, no surpliced choir, no flowers, no cross, no candles, only occasional celebrations of the Holy Eucharist – altogether a thoroughly Protestant atmosphere. Such were the conditions, and it was my intention before I laid down my office to see to it that the parish church of Heart's Content should at least possess the accessories of a decent service.[14]

This came as music to the ears of the Englishmen perhaps, but was not so easy for the rest of the congregation. The members of Aughrim Lodge No. 6 of the Loyal Orange Association, established in 1871 under founding master Charles "Long Charlie" Rendell, were especially resistant to the new regimen. Smith ran up against them straight away on his arrival when he tried to decorate the church with fir boughs at Christmas. Long Charlie was adamant that nothing green – the Fenian colour – be brought into the church, eventually backing down when Smith was able to point to scriptural authority for the practice.[15] But the Orangemen were further alienated when Smith refused to let them perform their society ritual at the burial of one of their members, and some left the church on the spot.

Most of the locals went along, if reluctantly, with Smith's revisions, but defections to the Methodist church continued and their membership swelled to 90 by 1884. They finished their parsonage in 1882, with or without an Anglo grant. To accommodate their growing numbers, they enlarged the church and added a basement in 1889. By this time a more harmonious atmosphere prevailed. William Dickenson furnished the plans for their extension, and the report of a Methodist missionary meeting at Heart's Content in 1888 noted, "One pleasing and noticeable feature in our meeting was the number of Episcopalians present. We could wish that such a spirit of unanimity were more generally manifested."[16]

Meanwhile, disaster struck Reverend Smith on a blustery February night in 1886 when fire levelled the rectory. Smith and his family escaped into the storm with just the clothes on their back. The congregation found itself in a tough spot, with the rectory uninsured and the church still not paid off. It was two years before they could make a start on a new rectory. The Smiths, in the meantime, continued to be dogged by the memory of that February night. In September 1886 they returned to England for a year. After another winter in Heart's Content they departed in 1889 for the more temperate climes of Woodville, Maryland. Smith later became rector of St. Thomas's, a high society parish in Washington D.C. that counted Franklin D. Roosevelt among its communicants.

Reverend H.C.H. Johnson, a bachelor from the parish of Trinity, moved into the partially finished rectory at Heart's Content. Johnson was an amiable, dithering sort, nicknamed "Daddy Johnson" by the children. The debt on the church was paid off during his tenure, but the rectory was still unfinished when he left Heart's Content 11 years later.

The Church of the Sacred Heart

The Catholic minority of Heart's Content, beginning with the Irish servants to the West Country planters, had been given little opportunity to practise their faith. In 1815 they were on the periphery of the Parish of King's Cove, Bonavista Bay, that encompassed some 500 miles of coastline. We can assume that personal encounters with a priest were infrequent. By mid-century Heart's Content was part of St. Patrick's Parish in Carbonear. But with no place of worship the Catholic families were only loosely organized and some drifted along to St. Mary's. A few of the cable staff brought them together.

In 1882 a committee of ladies consisting of Mrs. Phippard, Mrs. Coupard, Mrs. Austin, Mrs. Williams and Mrs. Wallace, all cable wives, began fundraising for a Catholic church. The Church of the Sacred Heart, located on the upper side of the road to Southern Cove, was dedicated in October 1886 by the Most Reverend Doctor Ronald MacDonald, Bishop of Harbour Grace. MacDonald had to beat his way across Heart's Content Barrens through a driving sleet storm, but despite the bad weather a large crowd awaited him at the Sunday morning dedication service.[17]

The Church of the Sacred Heart c.1930. *Courtesy Claude Rockwood.*

The congregation, which also drew from Heart's Desire and Turk's Cove, still lacked sufficient numbers to support a resident priest and had to rely on pastoral visits from Carbonear and Harbour Grace. As it turned out, they were not able to support the new church either, which was soon cut down in size. Even reduced, the little chapel charmed a visitor in 1892:

> Crowning as it does one of the highest elevations of the town, and directly facing the entrance of the harbour, it is one of the first objects that attract the eye of the visitor...Though of much smaller dimensions than the Anglican Church, and with less pretensions to architectural design externally, it nevertheless rivals it in its interior decorations...The arched ceiling is tastefully and artistically executed. The altar is painted pure white, with gold lines, and stands comely to the admiring eye. A deep religious feeling pervades the whole building, and the visitor to it feels himself hushed into a reverential mood and softened into a devotional feeling.[18]

In 1913, with the railway cutting through their property, the church commissioned plans for a new chapel just across the road. When the congregation dwindled to a few families in the 1950s it shut down altogether and was demolished in 1954.

One Lone Soldier

The Salvation Army first appeared in Heart's Content in 1891, striking a chord with a young cable operator dedicated to the cause. Newcomers to Newfoundland, the Army brought a religious style especially appealing to those Methodists nostalgic for the lively, unrestrained prayer meetings of their earlier days. Carried on a wave of unabashed evangelical fervour, the Army swept through the outports and attained official standing as a religious denomination, which, among other things, allowed it to operate its own schools in a government-supported denominational education system.

At first the congregation of St. Mary's, still mindful of the Wesleyan upsurge, did not know quite what to make of this new intrusion, but a congregational meeting in January 1892 found them ready to close ranks:

> Mr. Charlton asked who were members of the Church. Rev. Chairman stated that any persons who connected themselves with any other church or sect or enrolled themselves as members of S Army could not be members of the Church and pointed out that the Rector was not bound to bury a corpse simply because the friends of the deceased wished it. After some remarks by Messrs John Farnham, Gaden Rendell & others Mr. Charlton proposed, Mr. J. H. Moore seconded that persons joining any other church or enrolling as member of S Army be not allowed to use St. Mary's cemetery. Carried.[19]

No dithering as far as the Salvation Army was concerned. The Army's stalwart in Heart's Content was Charlie Ollerhead, a 20-year-old Anglo employee whose father had broken away from the Church of England and married into the Methodist side of the Hopkins family. A bachelor with some spare time on his hands, Charlie Ollerhead became passionate in the cause. He volunteered as secretary of the Salvation Army in Newfoundland and spent his summer holidays helping out at headquarters in St. John's. His zeal is apparent in a small item penned for the Army's Canadian newspaper, *The War Cry*:

One would think it an impossibility to have a public S.A. banquet in Heart's Content, the people seem to be so much opposed to us, but the Captain's faith ran high, and six of us took up our cross to beg (without a trial there's no denial), and the Lord opened the people's hearts and they helped us exceptionally well.

We have no real barracks here, and we tried to get a hall, but failed to obtain one. We had with us Capt. Hoddinott and Bro. Howell, with his cornet and guitar, from Carbonear, also officers from Hant's Harbour and Scilly Cove. We had a nice crowd. The musical jubilee went with a swing. I believe everyone enjoyed themselves, and the unsaved had another chance to get ready to enter into the marriage supper of the Lamb, but none would accept the invitation...We realized the nice little sum of thirty dollars...[20]

The Army held their first meetings in a fishing shed on the Rockwood plantation, nicknamed the "tar-pot," where they attracted a contingent of men from Scilly Cove. By 1893, the Scilly Cove people branched off with a corps of their own. In Heart's Content a new barracks was established near the Main Brook.

Charlie Ollerhead's soldiership was cut short by ill health in 1896. In March, the station superintendent advised that he take a fortnight off and noted that he would be wise to "discontinue his more active operations in connection with the Salvation Army, public speaking, shouting, excitement and late hours not being good for him."[21] Anglo's general manager in London ruled that his occupations outside combined with his duties were too much, and he would have to resign one or the other. Ollerhead worked on and off until June when he was diagnosed with tuberculosis. He died in November. Forewarned by the Church of England policy on burial space, the Army had secured land for a cemetery on the barrens just behind Rowe's Bank. Charlie Ollerhead was the first and only soldier laid to rest there. After his passing the Army failed to gain a firm footing in Heart's Content and departed for good in the 1930s. Today, their tiny cemetery with its single gravesite is the only reminder that they were ever there.

To go from one Church of England congregation to four functioning sects in little more than a decade represented a major realignment of the religious landscape of Heart's Content. The transformation

Charlie Ollerhead's grave 2005.

came about at a time of increasing population, which went from 889 in 1874 to almost 1,200 in the early 1890s, but was driven by the leadership of the cable staff. Making up about ten percent of the community, they totally reshaped its religious structure. The principle of "leadership by outsiders," prevalent in the history of rural Newfoundland, was never more strongly validated than in the development of the Church of England, Methodist and Roman Catholic congregations of Heart's Content. One wonders what progress the Salvation Army might have made had their leader not been a third-generation native.

Chapter 9

Sport, Art and Hard Living

> From an obscure fishing village, never heard of out-
> side Newfoundland, it became world-renowned, and
> has ever since continued in the path of improvement
> and progress, and is now invariably referred to as the
> "thriving settlement of Heart's Content."[1]

The correspondent for the *Harbour Grace Standard* in August, 1881, had reason to be upbeat. Heart's Content was undergoing a building boom. A new office building, a school and two churches had sprung up in the space of a few years. The Orangemen had just finished their new meeting hall. Housing was in demand and builders were at work on stylish new homes for the Anglo staff. And the town finally had a post office, opened in 1875.

Prosperity was showing itself in other ways. Mrs. Alfred Hopkins, recently widowed, was advertising tourist accommodation with a horse and wagon available for those interested in viewing the attractive scenery along the shore. In 1882, two shoemakers and a baker were setting up shop, and a butcher, P. Hogan from Carbonear, was looking to take up residence.

The recreational side of life at the station was flowering. While the billiards room and well-stocked library at Cable Terrace were exclusive to Anglo employees, the whole town could enjoy the cricket matches and curling tournaments. The same was true of other entertainment organized by the staff and their families – flower shows, art exhibitions, and variety concerts that drew crowds of townspeople. Heart's Content in the 1870s and '80s was not only a hub of global communication, but also a recreational and cultural oasis rarely seen in outport Newfoundland.

The displaced Englishmen found Newfoundland a sportsman's dream. Crimson-tinged speckled trout filled the ponds and streams, and during the run of brown trout and salmon the brooks were alive with trophy fish. The English introduced fly-fishing, a novelty to the locals accustomed to bamboo poles and worm-baited hooks. For small-game hunters hare, partridge, duck and a variety of seabirds were there for the taking.

In the fall of the year the cable men, accompanied by Mi'kmaq guides, forayed into the interior of the island. According to the *New York Times*, they were not at all reticent at displaying the results:

> ... the operators invariably return with their sledges and drays heavy with venison, hares, rabbits, snipe, partridges, and plover; after each success they are sure to make a point of driving through the two important streets of St. John's, with their sledges and drays brilliant with flags, and themselves wearing suits of sealskin, *à la mode* of the Laplanders.[2]

To help pass the long, cold winters the game of curling became all the rage. The game was first played in 1869, and by 1878 Ezra Weedon had set up the Heart's Content Curling Club with membership in the mother club of curling, the Royal Caledonian Club of Edinburgh. March of that year saw the first competitive play on the Mizzen Pond between the Blues, skipped by Edward Moore, and the Reds, skipped by George Charlton. In 1880, the club had 26 members and was looking to play St. John's, the only other club in Newfoundland. The year after, with a membership of 35, they ended the season with their own bonspiel, William Dickenson's Reds going against Sam Bailey's Blues,

Mi'kmaq Indians at Heart's Content, 1872. *Courtesy Mizzen Heritage Society.*

followed by a celebration banquet in the Variety Hall.[3] The bonspiel turned into an annual event, and the players lamented that there was no club in Harbour Grace or Carbonear to engage in competition. Heart's Content would gladly have met them halfway for a match on one of the ponds on the Barrens.

The February weather of 1884 created a smooth, clear sheet of ice on Heart's Content harbour, and couples on iceskates cast long shadows as they glided around in the afternoon sun. Dickenson was president of the curling club, and the Reds and Blues competed for the President's Silver Medal in a match that brought out a big crowd of spectators. The ladies were especially enthusiastic in cheering their favourite players. The Bonspiel Supper was another high-spirited affair with toasts, music, singing and carousing well into the morning.[4]

Curling dominated the cold months; tennis and cricket were the games of choice in the summer. When lawn tennis became fashionable, the operators made courts next to the office in a roadside garden rented from Ebenezer Legge. Spectators were not welcome at tennis, where the ladies took part, and a high board fence screened the courts. Locals were not permitted to peek through the cracks and knotholes while a game was in progress. But the clunk of the cricket bat brought out scores of onlookers on summer evenings. Cricket was also in vogue in other communities such as Carbonear, Harbour Grace and Brigus and all of them fielded teams for competitive play. In 1889 the Heart's Content cricket team travelled to Trinity for two matches, losing both to the local club. In cricket at least, Trinity still reigned supreme.

Heart's Content attracted purveyors of the visual arts, initially with rather bizarre results. In the fall of 1879, Ezra Weedon brought to town a young Polish decorative painter by the name of Alexander Pindikowsky to adorn some of the company's property and offer art instruction for the families of the staff. On completing his three-month contract (which reputedly paid an astonishing £1,000) Pindikowsky moved on to St. John's, where his money did not last long. Hard pressed, he put his artistic talent to work decorating a cheque for £232 with the signature of Ezra Weedon. The bank refused to honour it, and Pindikowsky tried again at a city drugstore with another cheque for £65. The proprietor telegraphed Heart's Content, found there was no cheque issued, and alerted the police. They arrested Pindikowsky that evening as he relaxed in a downtown coffee house, perhaps mulling over alternative means of raising capital.[5]

In June 1880 he pleaded guilty to the charge of forgery and was sentenced to 15 months in prison. His lawyer, W.J. Hogan, in a bit of legalistic bluster, wrote Weedon rumbling that he owed Pindikowsky £65 and tried to collect it toward his fee. Weedon was unperturbed: "...I do not owe him a single cent. I am perfectly indifferent to legal proceedings knowing that your client has not a leg to stand on. I can only hope that in the event of a lawsuit your expenses are guaranteed, if not you will find yourself much in the same position as the celebrated Dodson & Fogg."[6] (Dodson and Fogg are characters in Dickens' *The Pickwick Papers*, unscrupulous lawyers who are unable to collect damages from a client.) Hogan backed off. There was more from Pindikowsky, however, whose prison term produced an unexpected side benefit for St. John's, where he offered his painting skills in return for time off his sentence. Soon he was doing fresco work on the Supreme Court building. His artistry can still be seen on the ceilings of Government House, the Colonial Building and the chapel of Presentation Convent in St. John's.

Two years after the Pindikowsky affair, J.L. Blauvert, a landscape painter and graduate of the Boston Museum of Fine Arts, spent the fall and winter in Heart's Content. Wives and children of the staff flocked to his art and drama classes, and in March 1883 they mounted an exhibition of their work in the Variety Hall. Like Pindikowsky, Blauvert's short stay sparked an interest in painting that lingered long after he was gone. Abbie Charlton, for one, continued to offer her artwork for sale at church bazaars.

On the drama side, Blauvert's productions played to rave reviews. "Seldom, within the range of one's experience of out-harbour life, does it happen that experience comprises such a feature as that furnished by the entertainment to which we were treated here on Friday evening past,"[7] enthused the correspondent for the *Harbour Grace Standard*. The program was typical of variety concerts of the day, but Blauvert added outstanding stage effects. The "Overture to Tell," performed by Isaac Angel, piano, and S. S. Stentaford, violin, included an enactment of the William Tell legend with the famous apple shot. In another segment, Master Charles Bellamy sang "Little Nell" sailing on an imitation sea in a sailboat that was made to gradually disappear, leaving the audience "refusing to be conciliated, so pleasant was the effect."[8]

Throughout the 1880s, musical entertainment abounded and hardly a month went by without at least one concert on stage. Isaac

Isaac Angel
(1845-1924).
*Courtesy Charlotte
Crawford.*

Angel was the driving force behind the entertainment scene, working tirelessly on church fundraisers to benefit St. Mary's. One night at the Fishermen's Hall in 1881 saw over 100 people turned away at the door.

Then there were the dances. Festive celebrations, "times" the locals called them, starting with supper in the Fishermen's Hall or Orange Hall, sometimes followed by a variety show and always a dance. After the chairs were pushed back, couples filled the floor while the fiddler played for lively old English set dances like the quadrille and the lancers. Anglo-American held their own invitation-only events, a little more sedate, at the Variety Hall to the sound of Isaac Angel's piano and James H. Moore's violin. Fashionably dressed couples whirled around in the waltz, the mazurka, the scottische and the polka, ending the evening in a traditional last set called "Sir Roger de Coverly," an English country dance known in America as the Virginia Reel.

The staff got up a blackface minstrel troupe, portraying characters with names like Sambo, Bones and Beeswax in skits and popular musical numbers such as Stephen Foster's "Hard Times," "Marchin' Thru Georgia" and "Sound dat Banjo." The ensemble put together shows for the SUF, the Orangemen, St. Mary's Church, and other worthy causes. One of their concerts in the winter of 1877 ended with an uncanny twist. A few days before Christmas of 1876 the schooner *Flash* set sail from Harbour Grace for New Perlican loaded down with a merchant cargo. Captain Charlie Matthews and his four crew were all New Perlican men, anxious to get home in time for Christmas. It was not to be, for a fierce winter storm blew up from the northwest just after they left Harbour Grace and they never reached their destination. Over the winter the cable entertainers, billing themselves as the Mohawk Minstrel Troupe, staged a series of concerts in aid of the families of the lost seamen. It was during their final sold-out performance on February 21, in the British Hall at Harbour Grace, that the unexpected happened.

The night was heavy with fog when H.T. Shortis, the telegraph operator, prepared to close up his office a few minutes before 8 o'clock. Looking up from his desk he received the shock of his life when there, leaning on the wicket with his eyes twinkling and grinning from ear to ear, was none other than Captain Matthews of the *Flash*. Assuring

Shortis that he was no apparition, Matthews waited for him to compose himself, then had him telegraph the news to Heart's Content that he and his men were all safe and sound in Harbour Grace. Shortis escorted the captain and crew to the concert hall. Imagine the pandemonium when the door opened and in walked the five missing men, witnesses to a concert marking their own demise. The commotion was stilled only when Isaac Angel struck up the piano with "Praise God, from Whom all Blessings Flow."[9]

The crowd settled down to hear how the *Flash* had been swept out to sea and, barely afloat with all her canvas blown away, was sighted at the last moment by the *Iris,* bound from Prince Edward Island to St. John's. After taking the men on board, the *Iris* was driven south by the gale, making final landfall at Barbados. From there the crew went to Antigua to board the *Arctic,* bound for Newfoundland. And now, at long last, here they were. The next morning the lost men and the Mohawks walked across the Barrens led by a brass band, the blast of their coronets knifing through the frosty air. People from Heart's Content met them halfway and others joined in, with lusty cheering and muskets firing. At New Perlican came the tearful reunion, the hardy seafarers finally safe with their friends and loved ones.

Heart's Content of the 1870s and '80s prided itself on its standing as a centre of culture and sophistication. When it came to hard drinking, though, it had all the refinement of the raw frontier. In this way, at least, it was by no means unique. With cheap spirits widely available, and the common belief that beer, wine and liquor offered nutritional and medicinal value, the eighteenth and nineteenth centuries were times of unabashed imbibing throughout America. Tippling was bound to be prevalent in a place like Heart's Content where money circulated and, as Ezra Weedon's wedding bash showed, the seaman's tradition of rum swigging still held sway. The marvel is that there was not more trouble with liquor than there was. Examples, though, are not hard to find.

Sam Bailey related an incident in September 1869 that left a pall on the community when 52-year-old Jonathan Hopkins, a respected citizen and shopkeeper for Ridley & Company, was found drowned under his wharf. Sam believed that rum was the cause of it: "It was a very melancholy accident & cast quite a gloom over this place as nearly 2/3 of the people here were relations of his."[10]

In September 1876 the crew of the cable repair ship *Minia,* lying up in Heart's Content, challenged the local fishermen to a boat race on the harbour. The Heart's Content men lost and during the post-race revelry a few of them, "rendered rather boisterous by too much liquor,"[11] were called to order by the constable and the Justice of the Peace. Not pleased, they proceeded to Constable Rendell's house and demolished part of his fence. Summoned to court in Carbonear all were fined and their ringleader given a month in prison. The affair roused the community, with temperance advocates praising the actions of the policeman and others condemning the sentencing as too severe. There was talk of an inquiry, and a petition went around to have Rendell removed but nothing ever came of it.

Another flare-up over liquor arose in January 1879. As was the custom, the Fishermen's Society was scheduled to parade on January 1 and the Orangemen on January 6. That year a large turnout, of the order of 300 men, was expected for both parades. With so many in a celebratory mood, the two district Justices, James Gardner and Reuben Bemister, decided to ban the sale of liquor on both days. More rumblings ensued, bringing temperance and anti-temperance sentiments again to the fore.

Intemperance was by no means exclusive to the locals. In fact, it was the biggest problem Ezra Weedon faced with the staff. Most of the operators were diligent, committed men who took pride in their work. The job paid good wages, they had a lot of free time, and were well looked after with generous housing allowances and medical benefits. Once they adjusted to the weather, it should have been an enjoyable life. For some, though, the tedium of "pounding brass" took its toll. A system of fines instituted by the company to penalize operator errors added tension to the work environment.

In the bitter month of February, 1875, two off-duty men, N. J. Collins and James Scanlon, decided to break the monotony by heading off to New Perlican on a drinking spree. As night came on, they set out for home with two companions. Collins, too drunk to walk, had to be carried by the other three. Approaching Heart's Content, they stopped to rest and laid Collins down by the side of the road, where he became ill and passed out. The others picked him up and carried on, borrowing a slide from Richard Penney along the way. By the time they reached Cable Terrace he was dead, strangled by a piece of beef lodged in his throat. Collins was 20 years old. Weedon laid the blame squarely on Scanlon, "a rather loose character."[12] In three months he was gone from the station.

Weedon had more than his share of headaches with John Sullivan, the rambunctious Irishman who had married the widow of Robert

Ollerhead Jr., inheriting two children and contributing a number of his own. James Bartlett also drank heavily, leading to an early death in 1884. Weedon tried everything to bring the two around – cajoling, stern warnings, suspensions without pay, even threatening to put them out of the company housing. Nothing worked, and they were a continual source of frustration. But both were old hands with families to support, and Weedon could not bring himself to terminate them.

With others, he showed no such restraint. J.T. O'Mara was summarily dismissed for drinking and neglect of duty. Alexander Saunders resigned after a drinking binge, rather than face dismissal, and Weedon refused to have him reinstated. Arthur Courteen, trying to cope with a bad marriage, received two warnings about drink before Weedon terminated him in April 1880. He moved to the station in Sydney, Cape Breton, lasted less than a year, then headed back to London. His wife followed, leaving five young children homeless in Heart's Content. "He is bad beyond doubt," wrote Weedon, "but she is simply a disgrace to her sex, and a millstone around his neck."[13] Dr. Martin was another case. Reportedly a drinker before coming to work with Anglo, the move to Heart's Content in 1870 was an attempt to leave alcohol behind. He could have picked an easier place. He soon slipped into his old habits, his wife took the children and left, and by the end of 1879 Weedon's patience had run out:

> On November 29 [the] Sheriff from Hr. Grace served Martin with a Capias. He went to Hr. Grace with the sheriff. He returned the same night with his lawyer & they both got the worse for drink. I wrote him asking for resignation, which I got. Martin came to me two days ago, crying like a child, showing me a most pitiful letter from his wife as to the destitute state herself and children are in. He begged me to allow him to withdraw resignation and give him one more chance, but I couldn't do it. I have written to 3 doctors, one in Brigus, Hr. Grace & St. John's stating terms.[14]

Within weeks, Weedon hired William Anderson of Brigus, a "hard Scotchman ... thoroughly sober and steady."[15] Martin set up practice in Harbour Grace, later worked with the Newfoundland Railway, and became government medical officer in Labrador. He died in 1902 from injuries sustained in falling down a set of steps on a steamer at sea.

Heart's Content streetscape c.1890 showing Cable Terrace, the Orange Hall and one of the company houses. *Courtesy Alex Rowe.*

Ructions with the staff over liquor reached new heights in 1880 with the arrival of four operators from Valentia. Horan, Hamill, Wallace and Jones were hard drinkers whose antics disrupted protocol and wreaked havoc at the station. They ignored the curfew hour of 11 p.m. and long-standing rules against using the company boats and the billiard room on Sunday. Their carousing forced Weedon to lay down a formal procedure for neglect of duty due to drink: (1) a friendly reminder, (2) a heavy fine, and (3) recommend dismissal.

The new rules brought an uneasy truce, but the Valentia men proved impossible to control. The last straw for Weedon came on a quiet Sunday evening in August, 1881, when a chamber pot and its contents came flying out of one of the front windows of Cable Terrace. At the time, J. T. Collins, the caterer in the mess, had requested a new sitting room for the men. "A sitting room will <u>not</u> be provided," Weedon bristled, "things are worse in the mess than I thought ...This is my last memo on this. The next thing I shall do is turn the centre building into 2 married tenements, pay a housing allowance to the single men & let them fish for themselves."[16]

Finally, Weedon approached head office in London to have the troublemakers transferred. Horan was especially trying. He was a good operator, but "in Heart's Content the Orange feeling among the natives is very strong and Horan is a bigoted R.C. far on the road to Fenianism. He has collided with the Orangemen and will never have any peace here."[17] Horan and Hamill were gone in a few months, Wallace resigned the next year, and order was restored. Weedon vowed never to accept another operator from Valentia.

The unrestrained consumption of liquor was nourishment for the temperance cause and in May, 1880, Reverend Murray organized a branch of the Church of England Temperance Society. Murray was elected president at the first meeting, where 16 took the pledge of total abstinence and one person pledged temperance. The movement gained momentum. *The Permissive Act*, passed by the Newfoundland legislature in 1871, allowed any community to bring in prohibition on a two-thirds vote of the residents. Heart's Content introduced the so-called "local option" in 1882 and shut down the only licensed tavern in town. Surprisingly, Reverend Smith and Dr. Anderson, both temperance supporters, were opposed to prohibition. Anderson had already seen the local option at work in Brigus, where it did nothing to curb drinking and in fact produced the opposite result. The same thing happened in Heart's Content. As soon as the tavern closed, five houses, "shebeens" as they were called, were offering spruce beer for sale, boldly advertising with a spruce bough nailed to a pole in front of the door. As Smith recalled:

> For the next three years of the life of the Act we had a hectic time. At the end of the three years the people, disheartened, went back again to the old state of things, and again there was one licensed inn in the town, well-conducted, and under strict regulations, rather than five unlicensed places doing business both by day and by night.[18]

The shenanigans of the Valentia operators were a drain on Ezra Weedon. Frail, pain-ridden and unable to carry out his duties as he thought he should, his final years as superintendent were anything but pleasant. But he remained devoted to the company and resigned to his circumstance. In October 1881 he wrote, "I have been unable to get to church since Easter 1879, and don't expect to go again until

I'm carried."[19]   And again in December 1883: "I have looked upon the last three Christmases as the last I should see and yet I am still here within 8 days of another."[20]

Financially he was not well off, indebted to Alexander Mackay, the Southcotts and George Charlton. Fretting about the strain on his family should the company force him to retire, he began work on an invention designed to increase the speed of cable transmission, ordering in special tools sized to fit his tiny hands. He told Anglo's general manager that if it became successful "it ought to yield me enough to enable me to leave this most ungenial climate before another trying winter comes."[21]   In March 1884 he wrote that his invention might "make a little better provision for the wife and children after I am gone which may be soon."[22] In May he had to put the work aside, too weak to continue with the necessary testing.

Assistant Superintendent Frank Perry looked after the routine running of the office, but Weedon, working only a few hours a day, remained in control. His old bite is there in a scathing memo to Dr. Anderson in May 1884 accusing him of using drugs in his private practice purchased on the company account. Two days later he was shaken by the death of his only son, just four and a half years old, and there are no more memos.

On Sunday September 14, Heart's Content awoke to find the company flag flying at half-mast. Frank Perry advised London of the news:

> It is with deep regret that I have to write to you of the death of Mr. Weedon, which happened in the night between the 13th and 14th ... He had been a great sufferer for the last five years of his life. For the last few months he had been getting weaker, but no symptoms arose to cause any alarm until the morning of the 13th when he was seized with shivering and diarrhea and towards the close of the day became unconscious. Shortly after midnight he expired in the presence of Dr. Anderson.[23]

The funeral was "largely attended by all classes. Nearly all the officers and clerks were there…with others from a distance – all being desirous of paying a last sad tribute of respect to one who for so many years had ruled over them wisely and lovingly."[24]

With four life policies, his estate was valued at $17,000. George Charlton and Alexander Mackay were given preferential claims. Frank Perry commented, "It appears that Mrs. Weedon is not so well provided for as might be wished. When everything is arranged, it is expected that about £150 a year will be the whole sum at her disposal for the support of herself and family and for the education of three children and one by the first marriage."[25] Lily Weedon took the children and moved back to Topsail, where she died a year later at age 29. Her departure ended the Weedon connection with Heart's Content. All that remains today is a tumbledown, weather-worn headstone:

In Memory of
EZRA WEEDON
for 18 years sup. of the
Anglo-American Telegraph Co.
of this place
who died Sept 14 1884 Aged 45 years

This stone is erected by his friends and colleagues as
a mark of their appreciation of the uniform kindness
and urbanity displayed by him to them at all times.

Chapter 10

Hunkering Down

Ezra Weedon's passing in 1884 marked the end of an era for the cable station at Heart's Content. Weedon found Heart's Content a struggling outport and left it a prosperous, well-endowed little town. The central part of the harbour, with its office building, schoolhouse, stately new church and fashionable housing, reflected the influence of Anglo-American and its imported culture. Flower gardens, shrubbery and hedging adorned the company houses; chestnut, oak, sycamore and maples spread their branches, and pigeons billed and cooed. To the extent that the landscape allowed, the centre of town took on the appearance of a well-off English village.

With Weedon gone, Frank Perry moved up to the superintendent's post. Cable traffic continued to increase, but for now there was no further expansion of facilities or staff. The station remained a must-see, though, for tourists still entranced by the wonder of it all:

> There is a side half romantic, half weird to the life of the telegraphers shut in their workroom at Heart's Content. Day and night the messages of two continents pass thither, make their brief stay, then flash again their meaning to souls far distant on the old or new hemisphere. In storm and tempest, 'mid winter snows and summer blossoms, these men, working often almost within earshot of the crash of Atlantic bergs, interpret the gossamer characters traced in rise and fall along the mystic tape. The knell of death, the wail of sorrow, the story of fortunes made or lost, the tale of wreck by land and sea, the crises of statesmen, the record of crime, the cry of battle, are all registered in the tiny line which, passing the sun in his course, makes two continents one in their knowledge of things done and to be.[1]

The advancement of the community also gained note. "The town of Heart's Content, like a prosperous alderman, grows more portly every year," wrote a traveller in 1892. "Many are the private residences that

Heart's Content 1891. *Courtesy Alex Rowe.*

have been erected...in finished architectural style, and augment consid-
erably the ornamental appearance of the town." The stores were "well
stocked with merchandise, and there is scarcely an article in the hard-
ware, grocery or drapery line that is not purchasable at their counters."
Business was steady - "neither progressing nor retrograding."[2]

Such was not the case elsewhere in the colony. The ill-considered
efforts of the government of Sir William Whiteway to finance a trans-
island railway in the 1880s had brought a period of economic and
political turmoil to Newfoundland. Another decade of poor returns
in the fishery added to a soaring public debt, and a devastating summer fire that wiped out most of St. John's in 1892 made an already bad
situation worse. Leading merchant firms ran up huge unsecured overdrafts at the colony's two banks (where many of the leading merchants
were directors, blithely approving overdrafts for each other), precipi-
tating the bank crash of December 1894. Businesses lost heavily,
including the Hopkins firm of Heart's Content. With the colony on
the brink of collapse there was another flirtation with Canada, but
independence prevailed. One visitor noted, "no greater insult can be
given a St. John's man than to call him a Canadian."[3]

Whiteway sent his Colonial Secretary Robert Bond abroad in search
of financing to keep the colony afloat. Bond used his personal credit
to obtain a $150,000 loan from the Bank of Montreal. Additional
financing was secured in Britain, the government brought in a series

of austerity measures, and as the century wound down Newfoundland slowly began to dig her way out of debt.

Behind the seemingly exotic life of the Heart's Content cable operator, Anglo-American was facing financial difficulties of its own. The company carried a large capital investment on its books, accumulated during the failure of early transatlantic attempts, and its shareholders demanded regular dividends. At the same time, increased competition bit into the company's profit as new players came into the cable business. The Commercial Cable Company started up in 1884 and reduced the cable rate from 50 to 40 cents a word. Western Union responded with a cut to 12 cents, whereby no one could make any money. In 1888 the rate stabilized at 25 cents a word.

By 1892 there were 10 working cables spanning the North Atlantic, with the Direct United States Cable Company, the *Compaignie Francaise du Telegraphe de Paris à New-York*, Western Union and Commercial Cable all competing for business. Anglo held their monopoly in Newfoundland, but there were now two transatlantic cables running to St. Pierre and four to Nova Scotia with links to the United States. The new competition and the company's burdensome debt load brought a drive to control expenses, and the Heart's Content station began to feel the pinch. At the same time, cable traffic was on the rise: in June 1887 Heart's Content processed a record 94,000 messages. The men were hard pressed to handle this volume of work but the company refused to hire additional help. All hands were working overtime with few days off; little wonder that they were complaining of writer's cramp and eyestrain.

October 1889 saw 105,000 messages go through, and Frank Perry cautioned London that the men were being taxed to the limit. To add to the strain, the town was hit with another outbreak of diphtheria. This time Dr. Anderson decreed that an operator from an infected household posed no risk and was expected to report for duty. The staff thought otherwise. They still feared the contagion of the disease, and many booked off sick rather than risk sharing the workplace with an infected colleague.

This epidemic carried off 45-year-old Sam Bailey, who was stricken on January 13, 1890, and died on the night of the 16th. Such was the fear of the disease that, even though Sam was a model citizen, no one ventured near his house. Anderson had to bring in Dr. Allen from Harbour Grace to help tend the case. Sam's neighbour and co-worker, Henry MacKenzie, visited a few hours before he died. Perry reported that "excitement ran high"[4] in the office, and he had to send MacKenzie away for a few days. For Sam there was no time for mourning – he was rushed to the cemetery and laid to rest (a few paces from Ezra Weedon) the day after his passing.

These were trying times at the station, and the older hands must have looked back wistfully on the days of Weedon's rule. With the mounting pressure, tempers flared. In April 1890, a scuffle broke out in the office between MacKenzie and Dickenson. According to Perry, "Dickenson… threatened to horsewhip MacKenzie who provided himself with a weapon, a short stick about 2 feet long, and when a further quarrel took place…used this weapon with such effect that Dickenson's head and left shoulder were injured. Dickenson then summoned MacKenzie for assault and there was also a cross summons from MacKenzie." Perry did what he could to "stop the dirty linen from being washed in public"[5] but the case went before the magistrate who fined MacKenzie $30 and costs.

The workload continued unabated. "We have a good deal of Sunday work lately," Perry wrote in 1893, "for it is only on Sundays we can do certain things and the day at home SOMETIMES is a luxury – however, we are expected to go on, like the London cab-horse, until we can't go any longer!"[6] A new high-speed cable, the last to span the ocean to Heart's Content, went into service the following summer. Alterations to the office made room for the Wheatstone transmitter, a new piece of semi-automated equipment that sent messages quickly - up to 60 words a minute - via a perforated tape. Operators used a device similar to a telegraph key to punch out the tapes, which were then fed into the machine. Thomson's recorder was still at the reception end, its tape output cut into strips and glued to sheets of paper, then filed as a permanent record. Even with the new technology there was no let-up in the work. The whole operation was handled by 33 employees, eleven fewer than in Weedon's time 10 years before.

There was little now to relieve the daily routine. A fire in the mess damaged the billiard table in December, 1894, and it lay idle for two and a half years. Concerts were a rarity. A few of the staff started a new drama club that put on one performance before disbanding. Travelling shows provided some diversion, including the Kickapoo Indian medicine show and entertainment featuring the revolutionary new phonograph. Dickenson tinkered away and came up with a chemical battery that the phonographers could use to run their machines. It was, they said, "the simplest, cheapest and most economical piece of work in its line" that in the right market "would not fail to be appreciated and bring to its inventor handsome returns."[7]

Frank Perry resigned as superintendent early in 1895 and returned to England to take over Anglo's Liverpool office. His replacement was Charles Trippe, one of the originals from 1866, just back from a stint in St. Pierre. Trippe found the company relentless in its drive to control expenses: "I will undertake to reduce overtime and scrutinize every item of expenditure to save all I can," he wrote. "The six months I have spent here have been the hardest worked period of my life – 12 hours a day, probably more and 3 Sundays off…This is a very hard station but I will do my best."[8]

One of Trippe's first duties was to notify the highest-paid senior staff – Angel, Woodcock, Collins, Dickenson, Charlton and Sullivan – that their services were no longer needed. Only Charlton stayed in Heart's Content, taking the position of government relieving officer. The others packed up and left. Dickenson, widowed in 1886, joined family members in Massachusetts where he finished out his days with the General Electric Company. Isaac Angel, who had contributed so much to the entertainment scene in Heart's Content, tried to set himself up as a piano tuner, but eventually went off to Sydney, Nova Scotia. Sullivan moved to Prince Edward Island, Woodcock returned to London, and Collins went to St. John's.

Others left voluntarily, lured by more attractive positions with the competition. Trippe was frustrated, telling London that they needed a system of promotion to retain the good operators, otherwise the station would become only "a school for our competitors."[9]   Heart's Content was in fact home to the elite of Newfoundland telegraphers. Men like S.S. Stentaford, James Wilcox, John Ollerhead and a young Harbour Grace native, Bill Ford, were at the top of their profession, dubbed the "Knights of the Key" by their co-workers. They regularly worked the stock wire, transmitting quotations between New York and London on the speedy 1894 cable. It was a task that allowed no room for error. Ollerhead was the dean of telegraphers and was sent around to other Anglo stations as an inspiration to up-and-coming operators.

The time of restraint brought about a change in hiring practices at Heart's Content, as the company began to focus on local hiring. A few men were brought in from England at the end of 1892, but experienced telegraphers were expensive and the company began taking on Heart's Content boys as trainees, or "probationers," at no salary, working them up in a year or two to junior operators at a minimum wage.

Eight were hired in the summer of 1895. All were from cable families. These years were hard on Dr. Anderson, working to support a family of 11 with one boy away at college. In better times, his private practice had paid him as much as the company stipend, but was now mostly charity work. A man of changeable moods, he more than once tendered his resignation, then withdrew it, then worried that the company would terminate him. His health suffered, and he told friends in St. John's that he was having heart trouble. A young physician from Nova Scotia, Allen L. Smith, set up a second practice in Heart's Content in 1896, adding to his stress.

On January 26, 1897, Anderson made a morning call to New Perlican, returned home just after lunch and saw patients all afternoon. Depressed and distracted, he told his wife several times that he had something important to tell her, but never got around to it. That night he walked to Southern Cove on a call, all the while complaining of chest pains. The roads were icy but the night was clear and he insisted on walking home alone. He was found in the middle of the road near midnight, dead of a heart attack.

The position of medical officer went to Anderson's son Arthur, recently graduated from the University of Glasgow. He returned home in April to take over his father's practice. Allen Smith died after a short illness in December 1899, leaving the town with one doctor once again.

Approaching the close of the century, Heart's Content - and the whole colony for that matter – was in a desultory mood. The fishery, capricious as ever, turned in a disappointing performance in 1897 and 1898. The political scene in St. John's was in an uproar, the controversy fueled by a lucrative government contract awarded to builder R.G. Reid to operate the just-completed Newfoundland railway. The aftermath of the financial crisis of 1894 still reverberated through the economy. Belt-tightening measures brought a hunkering down throughout the island - Heart's Content included. This time the cable company was not much help; their belt was as tight as anyone's. The days of the "jolly dogs" of Cable Terrace were long gone.

Charles Trippe, good-natured veteran of the cable service, was not the man to see the station through a time of tight budgets and pressured staff. William Bellamy was. He took over when Trippe transferred to an upper management position in New York in 1897. Attached to the station since 1869, Bellamy was a kindly family man,

William Bellamy (1848-1933).
Courtesy Sr. Catherine Bellamy.

but a no-nonsense sort with a plain-spoken, dismissive air about him when it came to business. His advice to a young man seeking work as an operator shows how he ran the station: "I may as well say that this is a very busy place, quite unlike a government department. While on duty there is no time to talk and every employee is expected to do as he is told and no back talk."[10] Hearing impaired since a young man, Bellamy broached no insubordination, real or imagined. He suspected a staff member of complaining to the government about maintenance of the company's waterline, which prompted a personal memo: "Have you directly or indirectly made any complaint to the Colonial Secretary or any other government officials about the water supply?"[11] The unwitting operator waffled and Bellamy shot back: "When I ask you a question be good enough to answer 'yes' or 'no'. When your opinion is wanted it will be asked for."[12]

The staff did have Bellamy's support in lobbying head office for accumulated leave. Their annual one-month vacation was not enough time to allow them to visit the "old country" and Bellamy, who had never really adjusted to life in Newfoundland, was more than sympathetic:

> I submit no fair comparison can be drawn between staff in England and men in Heart's Content. The former can take a holiday even on a Sunday while their annual leave can be spent in the most charming places in England, Scotland, Ireland or on the continent at a moderate cost. 1. Remote backwoods 2. No society or amusements. That's your description of this place. The same remarks are true of the whole of Newfoundland, St. John's excepted. Its only attractions are filth and drink. It is therefore clear a man cannot spend an enjoyable holiday in the Colony and the time at present granted does not permit him to go abroad. The opposition allow their men's leave to accumulate 1, 2 and 3 months.[13]

At the same time, Bellamy confided that frequent trips overseas were not likely to materialize. "Dr. Anderson, F. Anderson, Scotland, Jr., N.F. Trippe, Bellamy, Jr., Cook, Jr. were all born in Newfoundland but they don't call it home. All their relations are in England, Scotland or Ireland, and they labour under the delusion these people would be glad to see them. One visit would probably effect a cure..."[14]

In the closing days of 1901, some Anglo employees might well have appreciated a little time away from the colony, considering the treatment their company was getting in the local press. The commotion centered around a new luminary just arrived on Newfoundland's shores - Guglielmo Marconi.

Marconi, a wealthy inventor from Bologna with a patented system of wireless telegraphy, landed in St. John's in early December 1901. He already had his invention working in Europe and was ready to show the world that wireless communication could span the Atlantic. This he did on Signal Hill on December 12, picking up transmission of the Morse letter S (three dots) from Poldhu in Cornwall. St. John's made him the toast of the town, and it looked like Newfoundland would again make communications history as the site of the first transatlantic wireless station. Anglo-American had other plans. On December 16, Marconi was met at the door of his hotel by the company's solicitor who served notice to remove his equipment from Signal Hill and discontinue any further experimentation.

Anglo, under Alexander Mackay, was moving to protect its 50-year monopoly on telegraphic communication granted to Cyrus Field in 1854. News of the legal action did not play well. Here was the last word in modern communication, certain to bring a measure of prosperity (or at least respect) to a struggling colony, being undermined by a monopoly with less than three years to run. Legal arguments ensued, the press railed against Anglo-American, and the company refused to back down.

On Christmas Eve Marconi boarded the train for Port-aux-Basques, took the ferry to North Sydney and accepted an offer of $80,000 from the Canadian government to set up at Glace Bay, Nova Scotia. "No one can tell what has been lost to the Colony by the action of the Anglo-American Telegraph Co. in interfering with Mr. Marconi when that gentleman was testing his system in St. John's,"[15] wrote the *Harbour Grace Standard.* Anglo continued to stand by their monopoly until it expired and only then was Newfoundland able to open its doors to other cable companies.

Marconi's humiliation at the hands of Anglo-American came at the end of some tough years for the company in Newfoundland. Now the economy was on the brink of recovery, and in the new competitive landscape of the cable industry, Heart's Content's light would shine bright again. Anglo, on the other hand, debt-ridden and without the protection of the Cyrus Field monopoly, was on the way out.

Chapter 11

Boom Times

As the new century progressed, Heart's Content again began to thrive. The station's probationer program provided new additions to the staff, and business for the shopkeepers saw steady improvement. White-collar jobs awaited young men who could finish school. Schoolmaster William E. Bradbury intended to see them filled: "My ambition and aim is to endeavour (by God's help) to give as many poor children as possible a liberal education – an education such that if a position offers more than a fisherman's pay they might be able to fill it," he wrote in 1903. He boasted to the Colonial and Continental Church Society that during the previous year "two of my boys secured positions in the cable office, and three others have situations in dry goods and provisions stores."[1]

Not many fishermen's sons made it, for in their hiring Anglo-American looked first to the families of existing staff, then to the children of merchants and tradesmen. New names like Hopkins, Young, Rendell and Rowe began showing up on the company payroll. For boys outside the cable circle, a job at the station automatically elevated their standing in the community. They entered a world of starched shirts and collars, proper speech and decorum, where everyday conversation turned on international affairs. There were privileges at the library and the billiards room. The young men ascended the social scale, married appropriately, and achieved a status that only Anglo staff enjoyed. In essence, they formed a working middle class, a social order found in only a handful of Newfoundland communities.

As the white-collar jobs increased, the fishery in Heart's Content went into a gradual decline. The annual voyage to Labrador gave a summer's pay for some, but others were putting aside their nets. The fishing stages remained, but fishing for a living was dying out and Heart's Content was becoming more and more a middle-class town. Shipbuilding no longer provided an economic buffer – there was little demand for schooners – and the shipyards were gone to decay. Carpenters from the docks had already found work in Canada and New England.

With the station hiring, though, Heart's Content showed every sign of renewed affluence. In 1906 the St. John's firm of Ayre & Sons recognized the growing market and opened a multi-faceted retail business known as the "Cable Stores," bringing city-style shopping, with home delivery, to the cable town. Organized sport made a comeback when a group headed by Anglo staff formed the Heart's Content Athletic Association. They brought together 74 shareholders, raising $800 in shares of $1 apiece, and set up a football (soccer) field beside the Mizzen Pond.

Football became the game of choice for young athletes, especially after a branch of the Church Lads' Brigade was established in 1910. Within a few years the Brigade, a paramilitary youth organization of the Church of England, had 240 young men enrolled at Heart's Content. They met twice a week for drill in military manoeuvres, marched in formation around the harbour, skirmished, and practised rifle drill and mock warfare. Led by Dr. Arthur Anderson, the C.L.B. developed a highly successful sports program, including an annual sports day. The boys excelled at football, competing with teams from St. John's and Harbour Grace for the Anderson Cup. Edward (Ted) Mallam of the cable station, one of the charter members, followed Anderson as the senior officer and captained the local company through the 1930s and '40s.

The station continued to hire, reaching 50 employees in 1908, all but a few of them Newfoundlanders. Still the tourists came, and still their wonder grew:

> Heart's Content is a dear little outport, straggling along the shore to where the cable company's red-roofed house and the fine dwellings of the employees, all red-roofed, and big windows filled with wonderful geraniums in profuse bloom, make a sort of central point. The cable men, in their long linen dusters, worked in a busy preoccupancy, their quick eyes reading off the tape message, cutting it and pasting it on a sheet with deftness born of long practice. One twenty-four hours' work, piled up in a room, would need to be seen to be believed.[2]

Jamming more and more staff into a poorly ventilated space led to recurring bouts of sickness, especially in the wintertime. The office environment became grimy and stifling, fouled by kerosene lamps burning through the night. In 1899, every household connected with the station was affected by either "la Grippe" (influenza) or pneumonia. Dr. Anderson and William Bellamy were both laid up, and Edward Martin came over from Harbour Grace to tend the sick operators struggling to work their duty. Still progressive in technology, when the opportunity came to replace the kerosene lamps with electric lights, Anglo jumped at the chance.

In 1900, Newfoundland's first electrical generating station powered up at Petty Harbour to run the streetcars of St. John's. Not long after that a group of investors from Harbour Grace, Carbonear and Heart's Content, including William Bellamy and other senior staff of the cable station, petitioned the legislature to incorporate an electrical utility. In April 1902 they established the United Towns Electrical Company, with a 50-year franchise to provide electrical service and – a lofty and none-too-practical ambition – operate a street railway in the three towns. It took two years to raise the necessary capital, but in 1904 they built a small powerhouse still in operation at Victoria just outside Carbonear. In November, the first electric lights went on in Carbonear and Harbour Grace.

The power line to Heart's Content went through in February 1905, placing the town once again at the forefront of modern times and predating electrification of most of rural Newfoundland by a half century. Anglo immediately replaced the old kerosene lamps. United Towns also put in a telephone line connecting the three communities, the first call from Heart's Content going through on February 4. The event was newsworthy, even though telephone service was nothing new to a town where the telephone had first appeared 27 years before.

United Towns Electrical Company supplied power under an exclusive franchise until 1919, when the Public Service Electric Company, formed by two breakaway shareholders, opened a 2000-horsepower hydro station at Heart's Content River in Southern Cove. Ignoring United Towns' franchise, the new company went head-to-head with them, signing up customers on the pretence that their service was for electric heat, not lighting. The two companies battled it out until 1932, when United Towns bought out their upstart competitor.[3]

In 1915, the cable town also became a railway town. The Heart's Content branch line of the Newfoundland Railway, connecting to the main line at Whitbourne, reached Southern Cove in December of 1912, extending to the terminus at the Mizzen Pond the following August. However, it was another two years before the station was

Train station and paper sheds c.1920.

ready for service. The first scheduled train pulled in on July 26, 1915, beginning a daily service to St. John's.

The railway attracted the Anglo-Newfoundland Development Company, who selected Heart's Content as the winter shipping port for their paper mill at Grand Falls. The company built four large storage sheds on the station grounds, and a 400-foot rail pier on Rowe's Bank. The first shipment of paper went out in 1916.

The town was booming, and by this time so was the cable station, finally out from under the burden of Anglo-American's debt. On March 1, 1912, all of Anglo's assets, including submarine cables, were taken over under a 50-year lease by Western Union. A well-funded American conglomerate with cable interests around the world, including a Newfoundland station at Bay Roberts, Western Union had the financial capability to alleviate the cramped quarters and overextended work schedules. However, it took some time. In February 1913 pay raises were approved for 47 of the staff, but the men were still disgruntled, especially the younger ones. Bellamy noted in a memo to head office:

> The next trouble will probably be loss of men. As you know, with the exception of myself, Tranfield, Richards and Scotland, all the rest of the staff are natives. Seniors satisfied, juniors discontented. As far

as my experience goes the Newfoundlanders are very difficult people to deal with.[4]

Of course Bellamy himself was not easy, which was part of the problem. On the other hand, natives who joined the staff no longer carried the deference typical of outport people. Having put them in white collars, the company had to deal with them on rather different terms.

With submarine cables now circling the globe, the telegraphic network encompassed all continents. Messages passed to and fro through scores of stations like Heart's Content, on tiny mid-ocean islands like Fayal in the Azores, Ascension Island in the South Atlantic, Fanning and Yap in the South Pacific, and Direction Island, part of the Cocos, in the Indian Ocean. The world of global telegraphy had many remote crossroads, and with each new cable coming on stream traffic rose ever higher.

At the time of the Western Union takeover, the Heart's Content station had seven siphon recorders, seven Wheatstone transmitters, and 36 perforators used to punch out the paper tape. In November 1913 an incredible 121,000 messages were processed, and even Bellamy was concerned: "We are doing a big business. Six cables worked automatically and only one spare transmitter which is cutting things rather fine."[5] Three new junior clerks came on in December, but they were still understaffed.

Word came from head office in New York of the company's plan to establish a school at Heart's Content to train new operators. Before the decision could be implemented, however, a major event intervened. At 7:45 p.m. local time on August 4, 1914, traffic on all cables ground to a halt, followed by repeated flashing of the message "CLEAR THE LINE! CLEAR THE LINE!" The duty operators watched aghast as a spate of official dispatches went through to all corners of the Empire announcing that Britain was at war with Germany.

The workload escalated at once, with no let-up. There were now about 70 staff, but every man was put on overtime, and everyone came close to doubling his salary. Charles Tranfield took over from Bellamy who, despite the war, lost no time returning to London where he settled into the life of a retired gentleman in the posh district of Mayfair. At the Heart's Content station the war seriously depleted the number of men in the hiring line. The idea of a school for operators surfaced again in August 1916 when Newcombe Carlton, President of Western

Union, came to Heart's Content, inspected the station, met the staff and went trout fishing. Tranfield wrote to New York in November:

> If the company wants men trained here, fix up a room in the old office, fit it with instruments and an instructor and take say 12 boys at a time from any school. Give them 3 hours a day without pay and see after 3 months if they show any aptitude. If so, take them in the station after 6 months at $10/month for local boys, $25 for outsiders. It is desirable that something like this be done as it is practically the only way to obtain men.[6]

By early 1917 Western Union was setting up schools in the United States to train telegraphers for the war effort and hiring women to replace enlisted men. In February, the Heart's Content school was established in the Variety Hall, used at the time as a clubroom by a local chapter of the Independent Order of Foresters, most all of them Western Union staff. To attract enough trainees, the company also invited applications from women. Women operators were nothing new to Western Union, who had employed them at American stations since the 1880s. The decision at Heart's Content, however, led to considerable discontent among the staff. They expected that hiring women would mean more demand for night work from the men and also lead to a lowering of wages. A deputation advised Tranfield that if females were admitted there would be mass resignation. The company's response was that they were going to proceed regardless, and the matter was dropped. Over the next two months 11 students applied – one man and 10 women. An application came from the Convent of Mercy in Brigus on behalf of six girls com-

Boys of the Cable Station c.1920. *Courtesy Department of Tourism, Culture and Recreation, Provincial Historic Sites Branch.*

pleting a commercial course. Tranfield enthused: "This is the class of student we require."[7]

With a co-ed telegraph school in place, the complement of staff shot from 80 in November 1916 to a peak of 210 two years later at the end of the War. Traffic on the cables was hectic, averaging over 800 words per hour. New Kleinschmidt perforators that produced the paper tapes for the transmitters from a teletype keyboard speeded up transmission, but more workspace was desperately needed. Some relief came when a temporary wooden annex was built to house the service department. (It was promptly dubbed the "service shack"). Then, in the summer of 1918, construction began on an 80-foot L-shaped concrete-faced extension. Western Union men came to supervise the project, with local carpenters working alongside roofers, plasterers, lathers and a coppersmith from New York. Come October 1919 everything was ready to transfer the cables over to the new wing, housing all of the automated equipment as well as a new environmentally controlled room for the artificial line. Teleprinters replaced the old siphon recorders, and a new time-division multiplex system greatly increased the capacity of the cables.

Building the extension to the station 1918. Note the temporary "service shack." *Courtesy Western Union Telegraph Company Records, Archives Center, National Museum of American History, Smithsonian Institution.*

Western Union operators at Heart's Content c.1920. *Courtesy Western Union Telegraph Company Records, Archives Center, National Museum of American History, Smithsonian Institution.*

Despite their commitment to hiring women, the company was slow to provide proper facilities for them in the workplace. There was no change area and in bad weather they were forced to sit all day in their heavy, wet skirts. Before the new extension went on, they had no lavatory either at the office or the school; the ladies were allowed a recess period to visit facilities at a nearby house. Even with less-than-ideal working conditions, though, the women learned quickly and performed superbly as operators. In fact, they handily outdid the men, especially in their keyboarding skills. Wage increases, awarded for speed and accuracy of performance, confirmed their superiority. Between 1917 and 1922, new female employees averaged almost $8 a month more than their male counterparts. Their wages, as high as $85 a month, were three times the top pay typical of working women in Newfoundland.[8]

The influx of new employees again placed housing at a premium. Tranfield was obliged to advise applicants for the telegraphy school that they would be admitted if they passed the medical examination, but the staff house was full and it was well-nigh impossible to secure lodgings in the town. The company started a row of two duplexes on the side of the hill overlooking the station, but with a shortage of skilled labour they took more than a year to finish. When the company house next to the Orange Hall became available on the death of John Ollerhead, it was converted to a ladies' mess, housing 12 staff and a matron. In 1921, Western Union underwrote the cost of eight new staff houses, mostly 2½-storey urban-style homes that further enhanced the well-heeled appearance of the town. To handle the medical needs of the employees, they built a small isolation hospital with an emergency operating room near Dr. Anderson's house. Marion MacDonald, a full-time nurse known locally as "Nurse Mac," came on the company payroll.

During the war years, with security tight at cable stations around the world, Heart's Content was designated a strategic installation. As in 1866, Western Union again rejected the suggestion that the employees be armed; instead, the building was placed under round-the-clock guard by three special constables. The senior operators also had strict censorship authority on messages going through. Efforts by the military in St. John's to recruit the men into war service prompted a visit by Tranfield to the Governor and Colonial Secretary to have the "molestation" stopped.

The period 1915-1921, with the station in rapid expansion mode and trains and paper boats running, was the height of the boom for Heart's Content. The affluent times brought a branch of the Royal Bank of Canada to town in December 1915. A Chinese laundry opened to keep up with the demand for clean shirts and collars for the operators. The Church of England school inspector noted that, "The demand of the Cable Company for big boys and girls carries off all of Mr. Bradbury's pupils at an early age; consequently this school cannot now shine in the C.H.E. examinations as it once did."[9] (The C.H.E. – Council for Higher Education – set common examinations for the upper grades in Newfoundland schools.) Once again the social scene sparkled with suppers, concerts and dances. Operator Bill Ford recalled the happy state of affairs:

> Traffic [at the station] was enormous; salaries had advanced to new high levels; overtime [was] obtained to a very liberal extent; considerable sums, from net semi-annual surplus, were as often handed back to the employees as bonus money and on two occasions during the "boom", the same good old Western Union…segregated very considerable blocks of its common stock for distribution to the members…as a "nest egg", at very attractive prices and upon remarkably easy terms.

Enlarging upon this plan, and in order to promote healthful exercise among the youth of the staff, substantial annual grants were disbursed to their Tennis and Athletic Clubs...[and] liberal fees donated towards the maintenance of religious and social organizations. The butcher, the baker and the candlestick maker had nothing to complain of. Orders were plentiful, and collateral not less so. Shopkeepers reported brisk business; in short every walk of life was lifted to a plane approaching Utopian conditions and it may fairly be stated that, for its size, the village of Heart's Content was the most prosperous, in a general sense, of any other settlement outside the capital city, and well merited its name "Heart's Content."[10]

Sadly, it was all too good to last.

Chapter 12

Final Days

With the end of the war on November 11, 1918, Heart's Content, riding the crest of an economic wave, had more than one reason to celebrate. Peace Night saw everyone on the street, stores and houses ablaze in light and muskets firing all around the harbour. At the station, humming like never before, the good times rolled on for a few more years. When the decline came, it came swiftly. By the end of 1921 cable traffic had plummeted to 25 percent of the volume handled during the war. By 1923 it was down to less than 10 percent, and new automated regenerators, which received incoming messages and relayed them on without the hand of an operator, easily took care of what was left. The payroll was slashed, with junior workers, including the females, the first to go. A few transferred to other Western Union stations but most left the service. By 1930 the employees numbered 25, with not a woman among them.

From a peak of 1,400, Heart's Content's population fell to 1,229 in 1921 and continued a downward slide. With the train running and the paper boats coming and going, the town maintained itself through the 1920s. A lingering echo of the good times showed in a steady stream of community events – dances, concerts, suppers, card tournaments of auction 45s,

Cable staff c.1930. Front row: George Bailey, Ed Hopkins, Raymond Hopkins. Second row: William Moore, Moses Rowe (seated), Steve Hobbs. Third row: Harold Martin, Evan Pugh, John J. Young, Max Young. Fourth row: W. A. Bonfield, Thomas Hopkins, T. Gordon Wilcox, J. Allen Rowe. Fifth row: Edwin Mallam, Bill Ford, Roger Tobin, Harry Rendell. Back row: G. A. Young, H. Ernest Wyatt.
Courtesy Donald Tarrant.

football matches in the summer. Both the Fishermen and Orange Societies were still thriving, and in 1921 the Masonic Order, with membership affiliation here since the 1860s, established Lodge Heart's Content with 19 charter members.

Bill Ford, a lanky man with boundless energy and a fondness for bow ties, took over from Tranfield as superintendent in 1927, the first Newfoundlander to hold the post. By now nearly all the operators were local men, a number of them second generation cablers. There were also many former employees living in retirement in the town. Through the 1930s and '40s the staff, both active and retired, carried on the privileged lifestyle and etiquette associated with the station, living in fine houses with domestic help. They kept up-to-date on world affairs, involved themselves in community organizations, and kept their own social circle. The company's recreation rooms had the atmosphere of a private men's club, a haven for poker and billiards. W.C. Palmer, an Anglo pensioner, kept the visual arts alive with a large output of watercolours depicting community life. Miss Oates and Miss Bailey, spinster daughters of former operators, both taught piano. The staff reactivated the tennis club and the wives took up bridge. Some of the women who had crossed the social barrier by marrying cable men were especially attuned to the social distinction.

Initially, Heart's Content was spared the brunt of the Great Depression. Western Union employees took a 10 percent cut in pay, but the cable office and the railway, though sputtering, helped keep the community afloat. Neighbouring settlements were not nearly so fortunate. With the bottom out of the market for fish, family after family went on government relief of 6 cents a day. In 1931, W.E. Bradbury, the former schoolmaster, was appointed special relief commissioner for the area. Men showed up for relief vouchers from all over the shore, boiling their kettles over open fires on the beach to make tea while they waited to see Bradbury. Some of them were utterly destitute, without even a kettle of their own, steeping their tea in discarded tin cans. On one day alone, in March 1932, 120 men showed up for extra rations.

Bill Ford retired as station superintendent in 1933, succeeded by William T. Stentaford, the first Heart's Content man in the position. Ford immediately notched up his involvement in community affairs. The Newfoundland government, in its final days before relinquishing control to a British-appointed Commission of Government, was promoting agricultural development through a program of community fairs. Heart's Content was picked as one of the first sites and Ford headed up the local organizing committee. The fair of 1933 brought in exhibitors from all over, showing off their vegetables, livestock, cured fish and handicrafts. Under Ford's leadership and with the help of many of the staff, keen to support anything that would keep some life in the community, it expanded into an annual event. The fall fair was one of the bright spots of the Depression years.

Otherwise, the 1930s saw one setback after another. The Cable Stores closed at the beginning of the decade. Paper shipments stopped in 1934 when the Anglo Newfoundland Development Company relocated their terminal to St. John's. The Heart's Content Athletic Association, its membership decimated, wound up its affairs and donated the football field to the Church Lads' Brigade. By 1935 the population sank below 1,000 and further layoffs at Western Union cut the staff to a bare bones complement of 15 men. There was no longer any need for Cable Terrace, looming over the street in its faded glory. The library and recreation rooms were moved to the office building, and the old apartments were demolished in 1938.

The next year the train stopped running. It was the final blow in a downward spiral and the people were not about to accept it without a fight. Organized by the Anglican clergyman, Hugh W. Facey, they rallied at the train station on July 3, 1939. Men and boys from up and down the shore joined together to block a work crew sent to take up the rails. What resulted was a peaceful demonstration by 1,500 souls, like nothing the town had ever seen, and it worked, if only for a while.[1] That fall, under pressure from the bishop, Facey was forced to disassociate himself from the movement, and the spirit of resistance waned. The rails came up in 1940. Local men scavenged what crossties and rail iron they could, and the once-bustling community bid the railway a final goodbye.

With the outbreak of World War II, the cable station gained a renewed significance. A round-the-clock police guard was back and security was tight, though this time the automated equipment ruled out any increase in staff. Indeed, the main function of the operators now was to keep watch over the equipment. Men departed Heart's Content to join the Armed Forces. Many more joined the civilian Newfoundland Overseas Forestry Unit, working the logging operations in Scotland that maintained Britain's wartime supply of timber.

When the war ended they returned to a subdued little place with fewer than 800 people and a lot of empty houses. Most found nothing to keep them there and moved on. Western Union took on a few to replace the older hands going out on pension. The company was now facing ongoing disruption of the cable service from expanded fishing fleets plying offshore waters. Stern trawlers on the Irish Banks and the Grand Banks of Newfoundland often hooked into the cables, bringing them to the surface. Rather than untangle their gear, it was quicker for the trawlermen to bring out an axe or hacksaw and cut the cable free. In April 1947, all four transatlantic lines were severed by fishermen, putting the station out of service for the first time since 1870.[2] The problem persisted throughout the 1950s and early '60s. The cable ships *Cyrus Field* and *Lord Kelvin*, on standby for repair work, were busy keeping up.

Meanwhile, the political side of life was heating up again in Newfoundland. Commission of Government, assisted by a buoyant wartime economy, had brought the colony to self-sufficiency, and now the country had to decide what form of government came next. Joseph R. Smallwood, a sometime broadcaster, writer, union organizer, political gadfly and an accomplished propagandist, used a well-honed grass-roots savvy to champion confederation with Canada. His colourful oratory dominated the debate leading up to the referendum where Newfoundlanders chose between a return to responsible government or confederation. When the votes were counted, two out of three on the Avalon Peninsula favoured responsible government. Not so in the rest of the country. The margin for confederation was 52.34 percent, and Newfoundland became the tenth province of Canada on March 31, 1949.

A few months later, on July 27, flags flew from the cable station at Heart's Content and automobiles lined the road bumper-to-bumper in both directions. The occasion, hosted by Superintendent H.E. Wyatt, was the unveiling of a special memorial commemorating the cable landing. The brainchild of J. McIntyre of Commercial Cables Ltd. in St. John's, the monument was a gift from the three cable companies operating in Newfoundland – Western Union, Commercial Cables, and Cable and Wireless Ltd. (formerly the Direct United States Cable Company) operating a station in Harbour Grace. The eight-foot granite slab draped with the Stars and Stripes and Newfoundland's Red Ensign – there was yet little enthusiasm for the flag of Canada – was unveiled by the province's new Lieutenant-Governor Sir Albert Walsh. Speakers made glowing references to Heart's Content as the "cable capital" of Newfoundland, site of "the

H. L. Benton of Cable and Wireless Ltd. speaking at the unveiling of
the cable monument, July, 1949. *Courtesy Alex J. Rowe.*

greatest event in Newfoundland's history and in the history of international communications up to that time."[3]

The ceremony was a nod to the past glory of a station in its dying
days, for transatlantic telegraphy was coming to an end. In 1956, the
first of a new generation of subsea telephone cables went into service
between Clarenville, Newfoundland and Oban, Scotland. Part of the
formalities of the cable laying had a bottle of seawater from Heart's
Content poured over the shore end of the cable as it left Clarenville.
It was a fitting gesture – before long transatlantic communication
would also be transferred to Clarenville. The telephone cables, with
submerged repeaters installed at regular intervals, were much more
reliable and carried a much larger capacity than the old lines put
down by Anglo-American. They were also trenched through the
ocean floor and safe from trawlers. Western Union tried to compete
by adding repeaters to their own cables but they were fighting a losing
battle. With the trawler problems persisting, they began plans to lease
voice circuits on the telephone cables.

At Heart's Content, the old cable hands saw no need for alarm.
Evan Pugh, superintendent during the 1950s, and his successor Eric
Stentaford had heard many rumours over the years about the station

Cable staff c.1958. Front row: W. A. Bonfield, Claude Hobbs, Dr. E. J. Short, J. E. B. Stentaford, Evan Pugh, Robert A. Mackay, Andrew Hillyard, Ralph Stentaford. Second row: Arthur Tavenor, Roland Peddle, Roy Cumby, Chester George, Ken Traverse, Mervyn Parrott, Basil Berrigan, George Janes, Frederick Cumby, Eric Harnum. *Courtesy Department of Tourism, Culture and Recreation, Provincial Historic Sites Branch.*

closing but nothing had ever come of it. There was a long tradition here to respect and a shutdown was unthinkable. The younger men hired to replace retiring staff had trouble sharing the confidence of the old-timers. They noticed now that when a cable went down there was no hurry to get repairs underway. No one wanted to admit it, but it became obvious that the new telephone cables would spell the end of the station at Heart's Content. One operator left for college and a teaching career. Another took a year off to study electronics, just in case.

One of the junior operators, Sterling D. Pike, an 18-year-old short-wave enthusiast from Carbonear, made some communications history of his own in 1960 when he brought together a group of listeners to form the North American Short Wave Association. They put out a bi-monthly bulletin and quickly increased their membership to 50. From a modest beginning the Association grew to 2,000 members worldwide at its peak in 1981 and numbered 850 at the end of the millennium. Its early history notes:

It was headquartered in an obscure Canadian town called Heart's Content, Newfoundland, which was the home of its now equally obscure founding president, Sterling D. Pike. Absolutely nothing is now known about Pike, who seemingly had resigned from any club leadership position by the fourth issue of the bulletin [March 1, 1962].[4]

At Heart's Content the station coasted along. Just as in 1866, the staff worked eight-hour shifts, two men to a shift, seven days a week. The company trained them in Morse Code, which was used occasionally on the service lines before the teletype replaced it in the early 1950s. They continued to monitor the automated equipment handling three cables from Valentia and four going westward, one to St. Pierre and three to North Sydney. The work was undemanding. The new staff had young families and became part of community life, playing an active role in church and school affairs and the Church Lads' Brigade. W.A. Bonfield, a native of Kent, England, was the station mechanician, there since 1927. He found little call for his specialized tools used in the old days to make spare parts for the equipment. A trained clockmaker, he spent a lot of time doing free repairs on timepieces and eyeglasses passed in at the station door.

Then, in 1965, the inevitable happened.

Harry Rendell, a former operator, first heard about it on February 3 and noted in his diary: "The butcher told us that he was told by [a Western Union] pensioner that the WU cable office was closing out shortly. I checked later with [the] WU employee and he said it was only a rumour as yet, but something's brewing…"[5] The rumours persisted. At the time all four cables were down due to extensive trawler damage off the coast of Ireland, and Western Union was weighing the merits of beginning repairs. As far as a closeout at Heart's Content was concerned, the company went into denial mode. CBC Radio in St. John's reported on February 12 that the Vice-President of Western Union Cables in New York had rejected rumours of a closedown of the cable stations at Heart's Content and Bay Roberts. "The company has no plans at this time to this effect."[6] In May the rumour mill had it that cable repairs were going ahead. Finally, on June 28, the decision came: "CBC News says that after 99 years of service the [Western Union] cable station at Heart's Content will be phased out and the 15 employees will be absorbed elsewhere."[7]

Responsibility for the shutdown landed in the lap of Superintendent Robert A. Mackey. A dapper man, soft-spoken, who wore his hat at a rakish tilt, Bob Mackey was a quintessential cabler. His grandfather, Robert B. Mackey, had been a young operator at Valentia when the first cable was laid in 1866. R. B. Mackey's six sons all followed him in the cable business. Robert, Bob's father, served on the island of Yap in the South Pacific where Bob was born in 1906.

The family moved to Brooklyn, N.Y., and as soon as he was old enough, at age 14, Bob joined the cable service. On the news that one of his uncles was opening a mid-Atlantic office for Western Union at Horta, in the Azores, he took a posting at the new station. There he met Blanche O'Shea, whose father managed the office of Commercial Cable. They married in 1935 and settled into a new staff house, tended by servants, to enjoy the pampered lifestyle – swimming, tennis and the social round. As their family grew, however, the Mackeys became concerned about educating their children in a place where the only schools were Portuguese. When they decided to relocate, the only vacancy available with Western Union was in Newfoundland, at Heart's Content.

They arrived with their three children to beautiful summer weather in August 1952. After Horta, living conditions here came as a shock. They were assigned one of the company houses of 1882 that had lain vacant for years, with no furnace, no floor coverings and no furniture. It did have an old kitchen stove and a sink with one cold-water tap. There were no servants. Blanche bought a washing

Bob and Blanche Mackey, New York, 1948. *Courtesy Blanche Mackey.*

machine but had no idea how to operate it. After appeals to New York, Western Union eventually put the house in order.[8]

Newcomers to a Newfoundland outport still needed time to adapt, as recalled by the Mackeys' daughter Kathleen:

> We were constantly reminded we were outsiders by our lack of understanding of the local usage of certain words. My father still laughs when he remembers how he reacted when someone said "Look at that fellow walking down the road with the machine on his head." He could not imagine what someone would be doing with a machine on his head. It was a while before he realized that "machine" could be anything from a hat to a sack of flour.
>
> My mother answered the door one day and a young boy said, "Would you like to buy a fresh fish m'am?" My mother asked what kind of fish he had and he said "Five and ten cent kind m'am." We did not know that cod was "fish."
>
> Apparently the company women were not especially friendly towards my mother at first, but eventually they asked her to join their bridge club and were a little more cordial to her. They also took advantage of her being a newcomer and got her to ask the station manager for use of a room at the office for their card club. She, being unaware of previous discussions over this point, did their bidding and was faced with a rather curt and abrupt reply from the manager.
>
> The whole family agrees upon the point that the general feeling of the town was that they took their time and sized us up before expressing any show of friendliness, but when they did eventually give in, they were for the most part, very friendly…[9]

In 1965, after a lifetime in cabling, Bob Mackey began the task of winding up Western Union's affairs at Heart's Content. Apart from the cable office, the company owned 10 houses, nine of them occupied, and seven plots of vacant land. There was also a carpenter shop, a concrete coal shed and the little hut known as the Fire House, used to store the fire hose and equipment.

Then there was the water system, and that was a major concern. Officially, there were 49 houses on the service, plus the cable office, the school, the Masonic Hall and the Royal Bank. There were also four of the original free-running hydrants, or "tanks," providing water for the rest of the community. Though the system was old, almost half of the line, including the 900-foot government extension beyond the Fishermen's Hall, had been renewed over the years. "The disposition of the water system appears to be everyone's concern," Mackey told the company, "but nothing has been done by the population to come up with the solution, formation of a Town Council."[10]

With the equipment shut down, the station itself was wrapped in an eerie silence after so many years of the constant clickety-clack of telegraph keys, relays and teletypes. For the first time, employees could hear the three old Victorian wall clocks with the Roman numerals ticking away. The men reported for duty, played cards, and waited to hear about their future. Eventually they were all offered positions with the company in New York and at a new station opening in San Francisco. They would have to become US citizens and, in a country at war in Viet Nam, they were also required to register for the draft. With mixed feelings, they all agreed to go.

The first four to leave - Arthur Tavenor, Ralph Stentaford, Gerald Green and Ken Traverse - took off with their families in August for New York. The others – Claude Hobbs, Mervyn Parrott, Roy Cumby and Chester George - left for San Francisco in November, along with Sterling D. Pike, the obscure founding president of the North American Short Wave Association. Pike, the only single man, was drafted. He finished basic training, returned to Newfoundland on vacation and was called to report for active duty in New Jersey. He flew to New York, decided he was not fussy about fighting someone else's war, and took the first plane back to Newfoundland, where he stayed.

The strain of uprooting the men and their families began to show on Bob Mackey. Arriving home from St. John's on a cold November night he came down with acute pneumonia and spent several days on the critical list in a St. John's hospital. On December 31 the closure was official when the last two employees, battery man George Janes and outside hand Fred Cumby, worked their last day. Harry Rendell, a 37-year veteran of the station through good times and bad, wrote, "It's a sad day for Heart's Content."[11]

Sad, because for three generations Heart's Content was known near and far as North America's premiere cable town. Since 1866, the cable had defined the community. Most townspeople had never been inside, or knew anything about how it worked, but the station had impacted the lives of all of them. From the beginning, the staff had moulded community life: churches, schools, recreation, housing, water services, the very look and feel of the town. The class boundaries had blurred over time, but the exclusive lifestyle enjoyed by the employees, resented by some and out of reach of most, lent a special character to the community. Closing the station removed a large part of what made Heart's Content the way it was.

In 1965, there were some who welcomed the closure as ridding the community of the remnants of the old class structure and removing control from the privileged few. No one could deny, however, the sense of loss. Gone were some of its youngest families, its anchor of employment, and its 99-year prominence in world communications. All that was left of the cable company were some vacant buildings, a few retirees and the memory of a glorious past.

Postscript

Two years after the station closed, on August 25, 1967, Heart's Content was incorporated as a Local Improvement District, authority to run the affairs of the town vested in a government-appointed Board of Trustees. Western Union gifted the water system to the provincial government, who turned it over to the town. In 1972 a new water and sewer service was installed, with hook-ups to every home around the harbour. The first elected Town Council took office in January, 1974.

The cable station, mothballed with all its instrumentation intact, was a natural choice for a communications museum. The idea was taken up by a citizen's committee under Cavendish native Herbert Bryant, the government welfare officer in Heart's Content. He wrote Premier J.R. Smallwood, on May 12, 1966, requesting that the government purchase the cable station from Western Union.[1] On May 18, Smallwood came to Heart's Content for the opening of a new Regional High School and met with the committee.[2]

Well versed in Newfoundland history, Smallwood was very much aware of the significance of the station. In St. John's he was contacted by Heart's Content-born Melvin Rowe, a one-time cable operator, now Regional Director of CBC News for Newfoundland. The two had a long-time connection through broadcasting, the Newfoundland Historical Society, and the Masonic Order. Rowe expressed his concerns about the disposition of the station, and Smallwood asked him to contact Edward A. Gallagher, president of Western Union International, to find out the company's plans for the site. Rowe made the call that got the ball rolling:

> A few days later, Mr. Gallagher, at the invitation of Mr. Smallwood, arrived at St. John's. Evidently he was very anxious to dispose of the buildings to anyone who was interested in buying them. The next day, the Premier telephoned me to say that Mr. Gallagher was satisfied to sell the property just as it was for $25,000. I told the Premier that in my opinion, while it was a good buy at that price, why not offer $15,000. And when Mr. Smallwood said he was willing to pay the latter figure, the company promptly accepted.[3]

That was in 1967. The following March Smallwood called Rowe to his office and asked him to chair a commission to establish a cable museum at Heart's Content. In the summer, two Americans showed up in Newfoundland, both with an interest in the history of cabling. They were Field Curry, an engineer working for Westinghouse and grandnephew of Cyrus Field, and Dr. Barnard Finn, curator of the Electrical Division of the Smithsonian Institute. After touring the stations at Heart's Content and Bay Roberts, now also de-commissioned, Finn asked to borrow some of the apparatus for a submarine cable and telegraphy exhibition being mounted at the Smithsonian. Through Curry and Finn, Melvin Rowe discovered that Bay Roberts was already well along with a museum committee of their own. He went to Smallwood:

> The premier told me that under no circumstances must the museum be located in Bay Roberts and asked me what I proposed to do. My answer was simple. Load up the commission with former Heart's Content cable employees and should it come to a vote, then the larger number would sway the commission. This was precisely what I did, and in consequence, the first meeting of the commission was held in the Confederation Building at 2:00 p.m. July 24, 1968. On the recommendation of Eric Stentaford the commission unanimously approved that the museum be set up at Heart's Content and not at Bay Roberts.[4]

The equipment went off to the Smithsonian. The cable commission met regularly, and Melvin Rowe continued an active lobby with government, at one point threatening to resign unless work was started on the building.

The project was no sooner sanctioned in the fall of 1971 when politics entered the picture. The provincial election of October 28 ended in a tie, throwing Newfoundland into a bizarre five-month period of recounts, burned ballots, party-switching, deal-making and backroom manoeuvring. Smallwood's Liberal government resigned in January 1972. Work proceeded at the station over the winter, but the unstable political environment put its future in doubt. The election of a Progressive Conservative government under Frank D. Moores on March 24 did little to allay the fears of the cable commission.

However, the new government came through with support for the project, and that summer the partially restored building was opened to the public. Harry Rendell, Western Union retiree and a member of the cable commission, kept a watchful eye on it, noting that 800 people signed the visitor's book in the month of July.[5]

Further renovations and the installation of exhibits took place over the next two years. The equipment came back from Washington, and on the morning of July 27, 1974, as part of the celebrations marking 25 years of confederation with Canada, the Heart's Content Cable Station opened officially as the province's newest historic site. Upwards of a thousand spectators and invited guests gathered for the ceremony. Stetsoned officers of the RCMP in red serge flanked the official platform, festooned with flags and bunting, in front of the station. The band of the Royal Newfoundland Constabulary played. There was no ribbon cutting. Instead, Thomas M. Doyle, Minister of Tourism, applied a pair of wire cutters to a length of cable, assisted by Barnard Finn and Field Curry, to declare the museum officially open. On the platform, a self-satisfied Melvin Rowe, along with Bob Mackey and other members of the commission, looked on.

The legacy of the pioneer station of the Atlantic cable was secure.

Dr. Barnard Finn, Field Curry and Hon. Thomas M. Doyle
cutting a cable to open the Cable Museum.

The Heart's Content Cable Museum Provincial Historic Site 2007.

Acknowledgements

This book grew out of research for a community history of Heart's Content, which led me to diaries and correspondence related to the cable station at the Provincial Archives of Newfoundland and Labrador. I was struck by the richness of the material, which contains not only technical and administrative details but also fascinating insights into the lives of the people involved. Reading it was like watching a drama unfold. Following up with newspaper research, parish records, copies of personal correspondence and interviews filled in the picture of life at the station and its interaction with the rest of the community.

I have many people to thank. I was greatly assisted by the staff at the Provincial Archives, the Newfoundland Room of the A.C. Hunter Library, the United Church of Canada Archive in St. John's, the Center for Newfoundland Studies and the Maritime History Archive at Memorial University of Newfoundland. Rev. Shirley Noseworthy kindly provided access to the parish records of St. Mary's Church, Heart's Content.

Many others provided useful information and advice, especially Bob Balsom, Alice Cumby, Dennis O'Brien, John O'Mara, Cyril Poole, Alex J. Rowe, and Otto Tucker. The following shared recollections of the cable station: Chester George, Hazel Goodridge, Neil Legge, Blanche Mackey, Sylvia Moore, Dorothy and Blanche Rowe, Margaret Stringer, Arthur Tavenor, and Frances Underhay. Catherine Dempsey, Susan Khaladkar, Patrick O'Flaherty, Paul O'Neill, Tim Rogers and Maureen Rowe took the time to read earlier versions of the manuscript and offer insightful comments. Susan Khaladkar suggested the title. Innumerable discussions with Tim Rogers, his detailed review of several drafts with perceptive critiques and suggestions were the source of many improvements. Throughout, he has been the inspiration and driving force behind the project. Bruce Porter convinced me to highlight the story of the cable station in a separate book. Many individuals and organizations also provided photos. They are credited where the photos appear.

The able assistance received from all these is acknowledged with thanks; any errors that occur are mine alone.

Abbreviations

AATC	Anglo-American Telegraph Company
CCCS	Colonial and Continental Church Society
CNS	Centre for Newfoundland Studies, Queen Elizabeth II Library, MUN
HCCS	Heart's Content Cable Station
HCSA	Heart's Content School Association
HGS	*Harbour Grace Standard*
MHA	Maritime History Archive, MUN
MUN	Memorial University of Newfoundland, St. John's
PANL	Provincial Archives of Newfoundland and Labrador, St. John's

Endnotes

Chapter 1

[1] F. N. Gisborne, "Journal of an electric telegraph survey in Newfoundland, 1851." Concluding remarks. Transcript, CNS.

[2] Gisborne's account of these events appeared in *The Public Ledger*, September 28, 1858.

[3] *The Public Ledger*, September 28, 1858.

[4] *Ibid.,* October 10, 1885.

[5] Cited in Gordon (2002), p. 53.

[6] For a discussion of the 5:1 conversion rate for US dollars to pounds sterling in the mid-nineteenth century see Gordon (2002), pp. xi-xii.

[7] *Ibid.,* September 28, 1858.

[8] May 19, 1857.

[9] *The Public Ledger*, September 1, 1857.

[10] Mullaly (1858) p. 278.

[11] *Ibid.,* August 13, 1858.

[12] *Ibid.,* August 17, 1858.

[13] *Ibid.,* September 28, 1858.

[14] *Ibid.,* October 1, 1858.

[15] *St. John's Daily News*, August 25, 1864.

Chapter 2

[1] Reprinted in *The Royal Gazette and Newfoundland Advertiser*, October 2, 1866.

[2] Munn, W.A. "Harbour Grace history. Chapter Seventeen – the Sixties." *Newfoundland Quarterly*, v. 37 April, 1938, pp. 13-16.

[3] Cited in Cell (1982), p. 86.

[4] 1753 census of Trinity Bay, PANL.

[5] Society for the Propagation of the Gospel, CNS (microfilm 471, v. B6, p. 182).

[6] Newfoundland census, 1857, CNS.

[7] November 23, 1864.

[8] Hutchinson's Newfoundland Directory for 1864-65, CNS.

Chapter 3

1 The quotes are from the *St. John's Daily News.*

2 *St. John's Daily News,* August 14, 1865.

3 Reprinted in the *St. John's Daily News,* August 19, 1865.

4 Reprinted in *The Times* (London), August 26, 1865.

5 Diary of John C. Deane. Cited in Field (1892) p. 338.

6 The chronology of events has been reconstructed from the following sources: Diary of John C. Deane, reprinted in *The Public Ledger,* September 4, 1866; Field (1893), pp. 339-343; Gooch (1892), pp. 142-151; Howley, M. F. "The Atlantic Cable." *Newfoundland Quarterly,* v. 23, December 1923, pp. 15-16; Moore, James H. "First Atlantic Cable." *Colonial Commerce,* v. XXVII, March 31, 1918 pp. 17-18; *St. John's Daily News,* August 18, 1865.

7 *The Public Ledger,* December 14, 1866.

8 Gooch (1892) p. 144.

9 Howley, M. F. "The Atlantic Cable." *Newfoundland Quarterly,* v. 23. December, 1923, p.15.

10 *The Public Ledger,* September 4, 1866.

11 *Ibid.*

12 *Ibid.*

13 *Ibid.*

14 Reprinted in *The Royal Gazette and Newfoundland Advertiser,* October 2, 1866.

15 *Chambers Journal,* v. 13, November 17, 1866, p. 726.

16 Reprinted in *The Royal Gazette and Newfoundland Advertiser,* October 2, 1866.

17 *Ibid.*

18 As quoted in Hearn (2003,) p. 235.

19 Field (1893), p. 370.

20 Gooch (1892), p. 183.

21 Field (1893), p. 371.

Chapter 4

1 Information on the operations of the cable station in this and subsequent chapters comes primarily from the diaries and correspondence of the Anglo-American Telegraph Company, PANL, MG 570. A copy of the early diaries is also available at the Heart's Content Cable Station.

2 Registry of Deeds, Companies and Securities, Province of Newfoundland and Labrador v. 17 folio 148 August 1, 1866.

3 AATC Diaries, September 6, 1866.

4 *Report of the Superintendent, United States Coast Survey, 1867,* Washington: Government Printing Office, 1869.

5 Bailey Letters, HCCS. Letter to father, April 25, 1868.

6 Details on the original staff are contained in AATC Letter Book, Weedon to Collett, November 23, 1869.

7 Graves, James "36 years in the telegraphic service." Unpublished manuscript, pp. 125-126, Donard de Cogan papers, MHA (MF-0126).

8 "William Dickenson Dead" *The Revere Journal,* September 16, 1911.

9 Bailey letters, HCCS. Letter to mother, Easter Eve, 1866 (transcription).

10 AATC Letter Book.

11 *Ibid.,* Weedon to R. H. Scott, December 6, 1867.

12 *The Public Ledger and Newfoundland Daily Advertiser,* February 7 & 8, 1868.

13 AATC Letter Book, Weedon to Collett, October 26, 1869.

14 *Ibid.,* Weedon to Collett, January 18, 1868.

15 *Ibid.,* Weedon to Collett, June 19, 1868.

16 *Ibid.,* Weedon to Collett, March 15, 1869.

17 Ford (1934), p. 47.

18 Merrett (1958), p. 150.

19 de Cogan, Donard "Cable talk: Relations between the Heart's Content and Valentia cable stations 1866-1886." *Newfoundland Quarterly,* v. 88, Summer-Fall 1993, pp. 33-43.

20 Bailey Letters, HCCS. Letter to father, April 25, 1868.

Chapter 5

1 Bailey letters, HCCS Letter to mother, January 29, 1868.

2 *Ibid.,* to father, April 25, 1868.

3 *Ibid.,* to father, January 18, 1868

4 *Ibid.,* to mother, January 29, 1868.

5 *Ibid.,* to mother, August 2, n.d.

6 *Ibid.,* to father, May 17, 1868.

7 *Ibid.,* to mother, August 2, n.d.

8 *Ibid.,* to Carry, August 18, 1868.

[9] *Ibid.,* to mother, January 10, 1869.

[10] *Ibid.,* to mother, August 8, n.d.

[11] *Ibid.*

[12] *Ibid.,* to mother, October 18, 1868.

[13] September 20, 1869.

[14] *Ibid.,* to mother, December 2, 1869.

[15] *Ibid.,* to mother, August 16, n.d.

[16] *Ibid.,* to father, May 17, 1868.

[17] AATC Letter Book, Weedon to Collett, January 13, 1869.

[18] Bailey, *op. cit.,* to father, November 2, n.d.

[19] *Ibid.,* to father, November 9, 1871.

[20] *The Morning Chronicle,* October 16, 1872.

[21] AATC Letters In, Weaver to Weedon, October 4, 1870 (clipping from *The New York Times* August 28, 1870 attached).

[22] *Ibid.*

[23] July 20, 1873.

[24] AATC Diary, July 12-14, 1873.

[25] AATC Letter Book, Weedon to General Manager, September 13, 1873.

[26] *Ibid.,* Weedon to Weaver, November 1, 1873.

[27] AATC Letters In, Weaver to Weedon, September 22, 1873.

[28] *Ibid.,* November 15, 1873.

[29] Bailey, *op. cit.,* to mother July 20, 1873.

Chapter 6

[1] AATC Letters In, Grant to Weedon, May 8, 1871.

[2] *Ibid,* Weaver to Weedon, March 21, 1874.

[3] AATC Letter Book, Weedon to Grant, August 3, 1871.

[4] Bailey letters, HCCS, Letter to father, November 9, 1871.

[5] AATC Letter Book, Weedon to Weaver, February 22, 1876.

[6] CCCS Annual Report 1876, p. 86, CNS (microfilm 619, reel A-634).

[7] Deming (1884), p.105.

[8] de Cogan, Donard "Cable landings in and around Newfoundland." *Newfoundland Quarterly,* v. 27, December, 1992, pp. 25-36.

[9] January 26, 1878.

[10] *HGS,* January 22, 1881.

[11] AATC Letter Book, Weedon to Weaver, January 11, 1884.

Chapter 7

1 CCCS Annual Report 1859, p. 94 CNS (microfilm 619, reel A-325).

2 *Ibid.*, 1868, p. 87, CNS (microfilm 619, reel A-327).

3 *Ibid.*, 1870, p. 73, CNS (microfilm 619, reel A-327).

4 *Ibid*., 1876, p. 86, CNS (microfilm 619, reel A-634).

5 AATC Letter Book, Weedon to Weaver, December 28, 1875.

6 *HGS,* December 30, 1876.

7 *Ibid.*, September 20, 1879.

8 CCCS Annual Report 1882, p. 46, CNS (microfilm 619, reel A-635).

9 Minutes of the HCSA 1882-1917, St. Mary's Church, Heart's Content. Meeting of April 1, 1882.

10 *Ibid.*, Committee Meeting, July 28, 1886.

11 *Ibid.*, Committee Meeting , February 26, 1889.

12 CCCS Annual Report 1886-87, p. 41-42, CNS (microfilm 619, reel A-636).

Chapter 8

1 Parish Records, St. Mary's Church, Heart's Content. Minutes, April 17, 1877.

2 *Ibid.*, Minutes June 4, 1877.

3 AATC Letter Book, Weedon to Canning, November 26, 1878.

4 Letter from George Gardner to J. W. James June 27, 1881. Society of United Fishermen, St. John's.

5 *HGS,* August 6, 1881.

6 Smith (1925), pp. 32-33.

7 Parish Records, St. Mary's Church, Heart's Content. Minutes, December 18, 1882.

8 *HGS,* October 25, November 15, 1884.

9 *Ibid.*, November 8, 1884.

10 *The Compass,* May 10, 1989.

11 Johnson (c.1925), p. 289.

12 *Harbour Grace Standard and Conception Bay Advertiser,* November 30, 1878.

13 United Church of Canada Archive, St. John's (Heart's Content Pastoral Charge Fonds, Series 5, Box 3. Correspondence on building a manse).

14 Smith (1925), pp. 35-36.

[15] *Ibid.*, pp. 33-34.

[16] *The Twillingate Sun,* January 5, 1889.

[17] *Ibid.*, November 20, 1886.

[18] *HGS*, August 19, 1892.

[19] Parish Records, St. Mary's Church, Heart's Content. Minutes, January 20, 1892.

[20] *The War Cry,* May 13,1893.

[21] AATC Letter Book, Trippe to Manager, March 6, 1896.

Chapter 9

[1] *HGS*, August 6, 1881.

[2] *The New York Times*, August 28, 1870.

[3] *HGS*, March 5, 1881.

[4] *Ibid.*, March 6, 1884.

[5] *The Morning Chronicle*, March 11, 1880.

[6] AATC Letter Book, Weedon to Hogan, June 3, 1880.

[7] *HGS*, April 21, 1883.

[8] *Ibid.*

[9] The story of the *Flash* is told in the Shortis papers, v. 4 (218), CNS and Ford (1933), pp. 15-17.

[10] Bailey letters, HCCS, Letter to father, September 20, 1869.

[11] *HGS*, September 23, 1876.

[12] AATC Letter Book, Weedon to Weaver, February 26, 1875.

[13] *Ibid.*, Weedon to Managing Director, October 25, 1880.

[14] *Ibid.*, Weedon to General Manager, December 8, 1879.

[15] *Ibid.*, Weedon to Weaver, December 22, 1879.

[16] *Ibid.*, Weedon to J. T. Collins, August 17, 1881.

[17] *Ibid.*, Weedon to Managing Director, December 31, 1881.

[18] Smith (1925), p. 42.

[19] AATC Letter Book, Weedon to W. H. Wiswell, October 30, 1881.

[20] AATC Letter Book, Weedon to J. H. Carson, December 17, 1883.

[21] *Ibid.*, Weedon to Weaver, April 23, 1883.

[22] *Ibid.*, Weedon to Prof. D. E. Hughes, March 12, 1884.

[23] *Ibid.*, Perry to Managing Director, September 22, 1884.

[24] *HGS*, September 20, 1884.

[25] AATC Letter Book, Perry to Managing Director, September 22, 1884.

Chapter 10

1 Deming (1884), p. 113.
2 *HGS*, August 19, 1892.
3 *Ibid.*, April 5, 1892.
4 AATC Letter Book, Perry to Managing Director, March 3, 1890.
5 *Ibid.*, Perry to Carson, May 12, 1890.
6 *Ibid.*, Perry to Dr. Muirhead, December 19, 1893.
7 *HGS*, May 18, 1894.
8 AATC Letter Book, Trippe to Manager, February 8, 1895.
9 *Ibid.*, June 10, 1895.
10 AATC Letter Book, Bellamy to W. R. Madigan, September 19, 1913.
11 *Ibid.*, Bellamy to Anderson, February 20, 1913.
12 *Ibid.*, February 27, 1913.
13 *Ibid.*, Bellamy to Manager, December 2, 1902.
14 *Ibid.*
15 *HGS*, January 10, 1902.

Chapter 11

1 CCCS Annual Report 1902-03, pp. 82-83. CNS (microfilm 619, reel A-639).
2 *Saturday Night*, August 19, 1911.
3 The story of the United Towns Electrical Company and the Public Service Electric Company is detailed in Baker, Pitt and Pitt (1990), pp. 173-205.
4 AATC Letter Book, Bellamy to Traffic Manager, May 1, 1913.
5 *Ibid.*, Bellamy to Fenn, December 19, 1913.
6 *Ibid.*, Tranfield to Walsh, November 7, 1916.
7 *Ibid.*, Tranfield to Traffic Manager, April 13, 1917.
8 Keough, Glen "Telecommunication pioneers: Women operators at Heart's Content." *Newfoundland Quarterly*, v. 40, Fall 2004, pp. 34-38.
9 Department of Education Annual Report 1919-20, p. 11. Newfoundland Section, A. C. Hunter Library, St. John's.
10 Ford (1933), pp. 82-83.

Chapter 12

1 *The Daily News,* July 4, 1939.
2 Diary of Charles Rendell, April 1, 1947, CNS Archive (COLL-295).
3 *The Daily News,* July 28, 1949.
4 "North American Shortwave Association History" www.naswa.net/history.html.
5 Diary of H. R. Rendell, February 3, 1965, Collection of the Author.
6 *Ibid.,* February 12, 1965.
7 *Ibid.,* June 28, 1965.
8 Interview, Blanche Mackey, February 3, 2004.
9 Martin, K. M. "What's in it for you, foreigner?", Student paper, MUN, March 1980, pp. 15-16, MHA (Nemec 0197).
10 R. A. Mackey "Buildings & Grounds – General – Heart's Content", August 6, 1965, p. 3 MHA (Robert Mackey Fonds).
11 Diary of H. R. Rendell, December 31, 1965, Collection of the Author.

Postscript

1 J.R. Smallwood Collection CNS Archive (coll 075 3.02.007 Heart's Content Cable Office.
2 Diary of H.R. Rendell, May 18, 1964. Collection of the Author.
3 Rowe, Melvin (comp.) The Heart's Content Cable Museum: Minutes and letters concerning its establishment 1968-1974, CNS.
4 *Ibid.*
5 Diary of H.R. Rendell, August 7, 1972. Collection of the author.

Selected Bibliography

Baker, M., Pitt, J. M. and Pitt, R. D. W. *The Illustrated History of Newfoundland Light and Power.* St. John's: Creative Publishers, 1990.

Cell, G. T. (Ed.) *Newfoundland Discovered: English Attempts at Colonization, 1610-1630.* London: Hakluyt Society, 1982.

Clarke, Arthur *Voice Across the Sea.* New York: Harper & Row, 1974.

Cookson, Gillian *The Cable: The Wire that Changed the World* Stroud, Gloucestershire: Tempus Publishing Limited, 2003.

Deming, Clarence *By-Ways of Nature and Life.* New York: Putnam, 1884.

Field, Cyrus West. In *Dictionary of American Biography, v. 6.* New York: Scribner, 1937.

Field, Henry M. *History of the Atlantic Telegraph.* New York: C. Scribner, 1866.

Field, Henry M. *The Story of the Atlantic Telegraph.* New York: Charles Scribner's Sons, 1893.

Ford, W. N. *134? Who is at the Key?* Unpublished manuscript, 1934. CNS.

Gooch, D. *Diaries of Sir Daniel Gooch.* London: Kegan Paul, Trench, Trübner & Co. Ltd., 1892.

Gordon, John Steele *A Thread Across the Ocean* New York: Walker and Company, 2002.

Hearn, Chester *Circuits in the Sea* Westport, Connecticut: Praeger, 2004.

Hodder, L.L. "Brief History of the Society of United Fishermen 1873-1973." Pamphlet, 1973. CNS.

Johnson, D. W. *History of Methodism in Eastern British America.* Sackville: Tribune Printing, n.d. (c.1925).

Jones, G. C. D. "Gisborne, Frederic Newton" In *Dictionary of Canadian Biography.* www.biographi.ca

Judson, Isabella Field (Ed.) *Cyrus W. Field: His Life and Work.* New York: Harper and Brothers Publishers, 1896.

Lindley, David *Degrees Kelvin: A Tale of Genius, Invention, and Tragedy.* Washington: Joseph Henry Press, 2004.

McDonald, Philip B. *A Saga of the Seas: The Story of Cyrus W. Field and the Laying of the First Atlantic Cable.* New York: Wilson-Erickson, 1937.

Merrett, John *Three Miles Deep: The Story of the Transatlantic Cables.* London: H. Hamilton, 1958.

Mills, D.B. "The Development of Folk Architecture in Trinity Bay, Newfoundland" in Mannion, J.J. (Ed.) *The Peopling of Newfoundland: Essays in Historical Geography.* St. John's: Institute for Social and Economic Research, MUN, 1977.

Mitchell, Sally *Daily Life in Victorian England.* Westport: Greenwood Press, 1996.

Mullaly, John *The Laying of the Cable* New York: D. Appleton and Company, 1858.

O'Flaherty, P. *Lost Country: The Rise and Fall of Newfoundland 1843-1933* St. John's: Long Beach Press, 2005.

O'Flaherty, P. *Old Newfoundland: A History to 1843.* St. John's: Long Beach Press, 1999.

Oslin, George P. *The Story of Telecommunications.* Macon: Mercer University Press, 1992.

Rowe, Melvin *I Have Touched the Greatest Ship* St. John's: Town Crier Publishing,1976.

Silverman, Kenneth. *Lightning Man: The Accursed Life of Samuel F.B. Morse.* New York: Alfred A. Knopf, 2003.

Smith, C. Ernest *Under the Northern Cross.* Milwaukee: Morehouse Publishing Company, 1925.

Tarrant, D. R. *Atlantic Sentinel* St. John's: Flanker Press, 1999.

Taylor, Bayard *At Home and Abroad.* New York: G. P. Putnam, 1860.